Children of Battered Women

Developmental Clinical Psychology and Psychiatry Series

Series Editor: Alan E. Kazdin, Yale University

Recent volumes in this series . . .

8: LIFE EVENTS AS STRESSORS IN CHILDHOOD AND ADOLESCENCE
by James H. Johnson

9: CONDUCT DISORDERS IN CHILDHOOD AND ADOLESCENCE SECOND EDITION
by Alan E. Kazdin

10: CHILD ABUSE
by David A. Wolfe

11: PREVENTING MALADJUSTMENT FROM INFANCY THROUGH ADOLESCENCE
by Annette U. Rickel and LaRue Allen

12: TEMPERAMENT AND CHILD PSYCHOPATHOLOGY
by William T. Garrison and Felton J. Earls

14: MARRIAGE, DIVORCE, AND CHILDREN'S ADJUSTMENT
by Robert E. Emery

15: AUTISM
by Laura Schreibman

18: DELINQUENCY IN ADOLESCENCE
by Scott W. Henggeler

19: CHRONIC ILLNESS DURING CHILDHOOD AND ADOLESCENCE
by William T. Garrison and Susan McQuiston

20: ANXIETY DISORDERS IN CHILDREN
by Rachel G. Klein and Cynthia G. Last

21: CHILDREN OF BATTERED WOMEN
by Peter G. Jaffe, David A. Wolfe, and Susan Kaye Wilson

22: SUBSTANCE ABUSE IN CHILDREN AND ADOLESCENTS
by Steven P. Schinke, Gilbert J. Botvin, and Mario A. Orlandi

23: CHILD PSYCHIATRIC EPIDEMIOLOGY
by Frank C. Verhulst and Hans M. Koot

24: EATING AND GROWTH DISORDERS IN INFANTS AND CHILDREN
by Joseph L. Woolston

25: NEUROLOGICAL BASIS OF CHILDHOOD PSYCHOPATHOLOGY
by George W. Hynd and Stephen R. Hooper

26: ADOLESCENT SEXUAL BEHAVIOR AND CHILDBEARING
by Laurie Schwab Zabin and Sarah C. Hayward

27: EFFECTS OF PSYCHOTHERAPY WITH CHILDREN AND ADOLESCENTS
by John R. Weisz and Bahr Weiss

28: BEHAVIOR AND DEVELOPMENT IN FRAGILE X SYNDROME
by Elisabeth M. Dykens, Robert M. Hodapp, and James F. Leckman

29: ATTENTION DEFICITS AND HYPERACTIVITY IN CHILDREN
by Stephen P. Hinshaw

30: LEARNING DISABILITIES
by Byron P. Rourke and Jerel E. Del Dotto

31: PEDIATRIC TRAUMATIC BRAIN INJURY
by Jeffrey H. Snow and Stephen R. Hooper

32: FAMILIES, CHILDREN, AND THE DEVELOPMENT OF DYSFUNCTION
by Mark R. Dadds

33: ADOLESCENTS AND THE MEDIA
by Victor C. Strasburger

34: SCHOOL-BASED PREVENTION PROGRAMS FOR CHILDREN AND ADOLESCENTS
by Joseph A. Durlak

Children of Battered Women

Peter G. Jaffe
David A. Wolfe
Susan Kaye Wilson

Volume 21.
Developmental Clinical Psychology and Psychiatry

SAGE Publications
International Educational and Professional Publisher
Newbury Park London New Delhi

For information address:

SAGE Publications, Inc.
2455 Teller Road
Newbury Park, California 91320

SAGE Publications Ltd.
6 Bonhill Street
London EC2A 4PU
United Kingdom

SAGE Publications India Pvt. Ltd.
M-32 Market
Greater Kailash I
New Delhi 110 048 India

Printed in the United States of America

Library of Congress Cataloging-in-Publication Data

Jaffe, Peter G.
Children of battered women.

(Developmental clinical psychology and psychiatry ; v. 21)
Includes bibliographical references.
1. Children of abused wives—Mental health. 2. Adjustment (Psychology) 3. Children of abused wives—Services for. I. Wolfe, David A. II. Wilson, Susan Kaye. III. Title. IV. Series. [DNLM: 1. Child Development Disorders—prevention & control. 2. Family. 3. Spouse Abuse. 4. Violence. W1 DE997NC v.20 / WS 350.6 J23c]
RJ507.F35J34 1990 618.92'85822 90-8212

ISBN 0-8039-3383-5
ISBN 0-8039-3384-3 (pbk.)

95 96 97 98 99 16 15 14 13 12 11

CONTENTS

To our three sons: Adam (PJ), Alex (DW), and Shawn (SW), who test our theories on child development on a daily basis.

SERIES EDITOR'S INTRODUCTION

Interest in child development and adjustment is by no means new. Yet, only recently has the study of children benefited from advances in both clinical and scientific research. Advances in the social and biological sciences, the emergence of disciplines and subdisciplines that focus exclusively on childhood and adolescence, and greater appreciation of the impact of such influences as the family, peers, and school have helped accelerate research on developmental psychopathology. Apart from interest in the study of child development and adjustment for its own sake, the need to address clinical problems of adulthood naturally draws one to investigate precursors in childhood and adolescence.

Within a relatively brief period, the study of psychopathology among children and adolescents has proliferated considerably. Several different professional journals, annual book series, and handbooks devoted entirely to the study of children and adolescents and their adjustment document the proliferation of work in the field. Nevertheless, there is a paucity of resource material that presents information in an authoritative, systematic, and disseminable fashion. There is a need within the field to convey the latest developments and to represent different disciplines, approaches, and conceptual views to the topics of childhood and adolescent adjustment and maladjustment.

The Sage Series *Developmental Clinical Psychology and Psychiatry* is designed to uniquely serve several needs of the field. The series encompasses individual monographs prepared by experts in the fields of clinical child psychology, child psychiatry, child development, and related disciplines. The primary focus is on developmental psychopathology, which here refers broadly to the diagnosis, assessment, treatment, and prevention of problems that arise in the period from infancy through adolescence. A working assumption of the series is that understanding, identifying, and treating problems of youth must draw on multiple disciplines and diverse views within a given discipline.

The task of individual contributors is to present the latest theory and research on various topics including specific types of dysfunction, diagnostic and treatment approaches, and special problem areas that affect adjustment. Core topics within clinical work are addressed by the series. Authors are asked to bridge potential theory, research, and clinical practice and to outline current status and future directions. The goals of the series and the tasks presented to individual contributors are demanding. We have been extremely fortunate in recruiting leaders in the fields who have been able to translate their recognized scholarship and expertise into highly readable works on contemporary topics.

The present book, prepared by Peter G. Jaffe, David A. Wolfe, and Susan Kaye Wilson, is devoted to the topic of children of battered women. The book considers the devastating impact of family violence on children, the links between violence and spouse abuse on child development and clinical dysfunction, children's views of violence, and strategies for intervention and prevention. Several topics are addressed, including methods of assessing children and families, obstacles in identifying the children, and the roles of diverse institutions and services, including shelters, the courts, and the schools. In addition to their review of several intervention strategies, the authors detail an intervention they have developed. They weave poignant cases, conceptual models of abuse and dysfunction, and empirical research to portray the scope of the problem and promising avenues of resolution. Overall, the book focuses on a topic of unparalleled social and clinical significance. The scholarship and sensitivity with which the topic is approached make the book a unique contribution to the series.

—Alan E. Kazdin, Ph.D.

PREFACE

Boy, 11, stabs man attacking his mother.

> An 11-year-old Scarborough boy stabbed his mother's common-law husband in the back with a kitchen knife early today after he woke up and found them fighting.
>
> He used a knife with a 9-inch blade on the man after he found his mother had been cut over the eye in a domestic dispute, police said.
>
> "I guess this child just couldn't stand seeing his mother being abused," a spokesman said.
>
> The 55-year-old man is in stable condition at Scarborough General Hospital with a punctured spleen and liver.
>
> Police did not name the boy, who is too young to be charged with a criminal offense.
>
> No one under 12 may be charged under the Young Offenders Act.
>
> Police said the boy was wakened in the Ellesmere Ave. apartment shortly after midnight by a loud argument between the man and his 28-year-old mother.
>
> "He saw them fighting and she was cut," a detective said.
>
> The boy went into the kitchen where he got the knife, returned to the living room and plunged it into the man's back. (O'Neill, 1989, p. 1)

This front-page story is becoming all too common across North America. Violence in families is a reality that cannot be ignored. Most often the victims are battered women and their children who observe this violence. Some children suffer permanent psychological scars from this traumatic life experience. Other children face physical injury as well when they are abused themselves or are caught in the cross fire of their father's violence. "I guess this child just couldn't stand seeing his mother being abused" is hardly an insight from a police spokesperson. Children cannot stand seeing their mother abused, but all too often this fact has been ignored by North American communities. This is the underlying reason for the writing of this book on children of battered women.

This book represents our perspective on the current literature dealing with children who are exposed to their father's assault on their mother. It attempts to integrate our own research and program development with this population by focusing on the children's special needs and promising intervention strategies. The first chapter offers the reader an overview of the problem and how the work on battered women and their husbands has naturally evolved to an increasing awareness of the indirect or unintended victims of this violence: the children in these families. Characteristics of these children are described in the broadest terms because the impact of this experience may vary greatly according to sex, age, stage of development, and a host of other factors discussed throughout the book.

The authors' views have been strongly influenced by our clinical efforts and research with women and children residing in shelters for battered women. We were constantly amazed at the courage of these women to survive a seemingly endless nightmare of physical and emotional abuse. Children's reactions were quite varied--from major adjustment disorders to average children who were apparently unscathed by the trauma.

We recognized, therefore, the need for a theoretical framework on how witnessing violence can play a significant role in child development. A child's need to have a family environment that fosters his or her emotional, cognitive, and behavioral development is contrasted with the experience of those who face extreme family conflict and disorganization. Predictions can be formulated on which children feel the greatest impact of this trauma.

Another important starting point was a review of the current empirical studies on children exposed to wife assault, which are based in large part on those youngsters who accompany their mothers to a shelter for battered women. These findings were compared with those on children who experience other traumatic events, such as physical or sexual abuse, psychological maltreatment, and alcoholism or psychiatric disorders in parents, recognizing that there is an overlap of symptoms and life events for these different child populations. Although research on children's traumatic events points to commonalities such as a posttraumatic disorder, this book also points out the unique aspects of children living with violence.

As we began our own research program we had an informal agreement with shelter staff to provide assessment feedback to mothers and to act as a service broker to make referrals to appropriate community agencies. We constantly thought about the practical implications of our findings in regard to assessment and treatment planning. Chapter 4 addresses some of the complex problems in assessing the extent to which children have been exposed to various forms of violence and the impact of this experience on child and adolescent adjustment.

The book also outlines the specific issues that confront children of battered women in terms of their own attitudes about violence. From the first disagreement in the playground to their own dating experiences, these children will have to cope with the clear messages they have learned about violence, conflict resolution, and power. Children exposed to violence also face questions regarding responsibility for this behavior. Is it their fault? Can they do anything to prevent the violence and protect their mother and siblings? These questions often find inappropriate answers that further trap these children into a sense of hopelessness and isolation. This volume addresses the issues in a broad, societal context that reinforces images of violence and supports children in the lessons about power and control. For example, violent sports heroes, rock videos, movies, and television programs may offer few alternative role models and, in fact, create a double dose effect of exposure to violence.

Chapter 4 also delineates the special challenges facing social service and mental health professionals in identifying and assessing the needs of children living with violent fathers. Interview strategies around disclosure of violence are suggested. A specialized child interview is outlined that may complement other assessment strategies.

Chapter 4 provides a focus on intervention planning for child witnesses to wife assault. Interventions are discussed from the crisis point when children are admitted to a shelter to more structured programs such as group counseling for children exposed to violence. Our program model is discussed in detail with some encouraging results from our preliminary evaluation of its effectiveness. A central theme throughout the chapter is the importance of helping children know that they are not alone in coping with this trauma. Other children experience similar crises and can offer support. Counseling from adults who offer safety and security may be essential when the plight of the adult victim is also recognized.

The final chapter offers some hopeful ideas for the future in consideration of the changes beginning to shape many children's services in this field. The rapid development of specialized staff and programs in the shelters for battered women is an important starting point. Limited mandates brought on by poor funding and inadequate staffing levels have now been broadened to acknowledge the significant needs of these children. Other agencies have increased their awareness of this issue and how it may affect their clients. Children's mental health centers have begun to ask the questions about wife assault that had all too often been overlooked in traditional assessment and treatment programs. Child protection agencies have widened their definition of abuse to look beyond the physical scars and recognize the emotional abuse of living with violence. The chapter discusses the importance of a reasoned response to this problem without further victimizing children by removing them from sources of support/family. Also outlined are ways in which the justice system must respond to this new awareness by recognizing the ongoing issue of wife assault after separation and during custody and access disputes.

The book ends by highlighting primary prevention programs and the potential of the education system to become a significant partner in a meaningful community response to wife assault. The authors hold great hope for workshops on teacher awareness of this issue and exciting new curricula that have been developed for all students from the primary grades to secondary school. We are encouraged by the many pilot programs we have reviewed and our own efforts that have been supported at a provincial level. Although this book and our own research program grew out of frustration in dealing with generations of violence and wife assault, we conclude that unlimited opportunities exist for primary prevention. In every classroom there exist potential victims and batterers. Their classmates will include their future neighbors, police officers, emergency room nurses, judges, and so on, who can all benefit from programs promoting new attitudes against violence in the family and a conspiracy of silence. We are optimistic that countless other concerned professionals will share our vision.

This book was made possible by several grants from the Ontario Ministry of Community and Social Services. These grants allowed us to research the impact on children of witnessing wife assault and the development of specialized intervention programs for this population. More recently, we have been able to conduct community workshops for professionals in this field that have helped to shape our thinking on the implications of our research. We benefited from the experience and wisdom of many shelter staff in Southwestern Ontario. In particular, London, Chatham, Cambridge, and Woodstock shelters provided a high level of support and encouragement for our efforts.

Social workers who offered a great deal of expertise in developing group counseling programs deserve our acknowledgment. In particular, Sheila Cameron of the London Family Court Clinic and Peter Lehmann of Madame Vanier Children's Services were important contributors of fresh ideas for intervention strategies. Finally, Deb Reitzel completed an incredible task in organizing references and summaries of key material in preparation for our writing. This book represents the kind and amount of collaborative work that children of battered women need and deserve.

1

DEFINITION AND SCOPE OF THE PROBLEM

HISTORICAL PERSPECTIVE ON CHILDREN FROM VIOLENT HOMES

The last two decades have been marked by a growing public awareness of wife assault or wife beating. The belief that all family life is safe and secure has been shattered by those who have pointed out the alarming frequency of various violent incidents in many North American families. This topic was once considered either a family secret or acceptable behavior within a patriarchal society. Extensive research by social scientists has suggested that family violence is widespread and is interwoven with the very fabric of society's attitudes and values (e.g., Gelles & Straus, 1988). Now, graphic media coverage of celebrated cases and regular discussions on the most widely seen television programs are commonplace (Toufexis, 1987).

A recent analysis by *Time* magazine on 464 Americans killed by guns in one ("typical") week (May 1-7, 1989) pointed out that the vast majority of homicide victims were murdered by family members:

> The pattern in these 464 deaths is depressingly clear: guns most often kill the people who own them or people whom the owners know well. Despite the outcry over street gangs and drug dealers, the week's homicides typically involve people who loved, or hated, each other—spouses, relatives, or close acquaintances. ("Seven Deadly Days," 1989, p. 11)

Although several important books were published on the topic of wife assault in the 1970s, very few researchers considered the impact of this behavior on the children who witness this violence. Most of the early literature in this field focused on the incidence of violence against women and the inadequate response of community agencies represented by the justice, health, and social service systems (Walker, 1979). The needs of children in these families were rarely considered. Except when children were physically abused as well, they were considered by service providers to be part of the battered woman's responsibility and added to the complexity of finding safety, appropriate housing, and financial support.

Case studies of battered women and their families in the initial literature in this field often made indirect references to the children and began to suggest several areas of concern. These included the following beliefs:

- A boy who witnesses his father assaulting his mother is learning that violence is acceptable behavior that is an integral part of intimate relationships.
- A girl who witnesses her mother being assaulted by her father is learning about victimization and the extent to which men can utilize violence and fear to exert power and control over family members.
- Boys and girls who live with violence are experiencing significant emotional trauma. Rather than having a family that can offer security and nurturance for their positive development, these children experience fear, anxiety, confusion, anger, and the disruptions in lives that are the aftermath of violent episodes. More recently, these experiences and their consequences are being labeled by many child abuse specialists as emotional abuse or psychological maltreatment (e.g. Brassard, Germain, & Hart, 1987).

When the concept of children witnessing their mother being assaulted is discussed, it is important to have some definition and frame of reference for the terms *assault* and *witness*. Defining *assault* is no simple task because, as Gelles and Straus (1988, p. 57) have succinctly pointed out,

> Twenty years of discussion, debate, and action have led us to conclude that there will never be an accepted or acceptable definition of abuse, because abuse is not a scientific or clinical term. Rather, it is a political concept. Abuse is essentially any act that is considered deviant or harmful by a group large enough or with sufficient political power to enforce the definition.

Recognizing this dilemma, we accept Dutton's (1988, p. 1) view that wife assault is any "physical act of aggression by a man against a woman with whom he is in an intimate relationship." In our view, this act may or may not be fully intended to cause injury or to maintain power and control. Although this work focuses on physical abuse of women, because of the concrete definitions sought by courts and shelter funders, it is acknowledged that emotional abuse that degrades and belittles women is an equally important area of study. The Conflict Tactics Scale developed by Straus and his colleagues has been utilized as the best available description for specific acts of verbal and physical aggression (Straus, Gelles, & Steinmetz, 1980).

When this study refers to children witnessing violence directed at their mothers, a wide range of experiences is encompassed. Children may observe this violence directly by seeing their father (or another intimate partner of their mother) threaten or hit their mother. They may overhear this behavior from another part of their residence, such as their own bedroom. Children may be exposed to the results of this violence without hearing or seeing the commission of any aggressive act. For example, children may see the bruises or other injuries clearly visible on their mother or the emotional consequences of fear, hurt, and intimidation that may be very apparent to them. Less commonly, children may be exposed to isolated incidents of violence, although these cases are unlikely to come to the attention of police or other social service professionals. Thus the phrase *children of battered women* refers to children who have repeatedly witnessed severe acts of emotional and physical abuse directed at their mother by her intimate partner. In too many cases, these children have observed repeated acts of violence perpetrated by multiple partners throughout their entire childhood.

Witnessing wife assault can have a broad range of effects on children. As Carlson (1984) has indicated, the initial knowledge about the impact on children of witnessing wife assault was developed through several areas of literature, including the impact of parental conflict, retrospective accounts of battered women and their husbands, anecdotal reports, and early studies on shelters for battered women.

Literature on the impact of divorce and separation on children (see review by Emery, 1982) suggested that the most significant stressor for children was the amount of conflict to which they were exposed. Even though it may be assumed that the most serious form of marital conflict involves physical and emotional abuse, the nature of such conflict was never detailed in these studies. Research focusing on childhood adjustment and the search for predictors of behavioral and emotional problems has also paralleled these findings on marital conflict. For example, researchers have identified a host of factors that usually include parental conflict and family dysfunction as predictors of child adjustment problems (Rutter, 1979). Had Straus and his colleagues at the Family Violence Research Center at the University of New Hampshire been involved in this research, and more specific measures such as the Conflict Tactics Scale been utilized, parental conflict and family dysfunction would likely have emerged as significant components, or "byproducts," of wife assault.

Retrospective accounts of battered women and their husbands often point out childhoods marked by witnessing their fathers' violence. Women who are battered often report that they came to expect violence in their marriage and saw very few options to end the violence (Roy, 1977). Batterers themselves acknowledge the learning experiences in their childhood when their fathers taught them how to be men and how to be husbands.

These retrospective accounts have been validated in later research that indicates that the vast majority of batterers have witnessed this behavior in their families of origin and that the rate of wife beating is dramatically higher for sons of batterers compared with sons of nonviolent fathers (Straus et al., 1980). However, not all sons growing up in violent homes become batterers, and in fact many siblings of batterers may live peacefully in nonviolent marriages (Dobash & Dobash, 1979). Retrospective studies of victims and batterers were a vital starting point in focusing on children in these families. The more complex research questions regarding children's immediate and long-term adjustment will be left to future chapters.

Anecdotal reports offered some vivid descriptions of children's experiences in a violent home. Even in the earliest books on the topic of wife assault, authors were cognizant of the plight of these children. For example, Davidson in his 1978 book *Conjugal Crime* captured this victimization:

> The witnessing children are the most pathetic victims of conjugal crime because their childhood conditioning will color their entire lives. All other input will be processed through the mire of the first marriage they ever saw and their earliest role models of husband and wife, father and mother. Daddy is cruel to mommy, who can't do anything to change it. No one seems to care, neither in the house nor out in society. The nightmare apparently is to be regarded as natural—or nonexistent—since it is neither acknowledged nor alleviated. To the child growing up in this environment, it seems as if all power is on the side of the wrongdoer. Nice people finish last. Perhaps wrong is right, after all. (Davidson, 1978, p. 117)

The phenomenon of children witnessing violence covers a wide extreme, from listening to the violence from their bedrooms to being forced to watch their mother being abused by their father as a lesson in fear and control:

> Oh yes, they've seen me be hit. He used to delight in lifting them up out their beds so they could watch. And this was 2 a.m. and he sat on the chair and told me everything he thought about me and he dragged the full three kids out of their beds and made them all sit. He lined them right up against the couch and told them all what I was. He says to them, "Now you see her, she's a

> whore." And he'd say to Chris, "See her, she's a cow." And the baby was only months old, and he'd say to him, "See her, she's no good. She's dirt. That's what women are. They're all dirt. There's your daddy been out working all day and that's no tea ready for him. See how rotten she is to your daddy." And all the children were dragged out of their beds for no reason at all. (Dobash & Dobash, 1979, p. 151)

Early studies on shelters for battered women began to identify the needs of children who accompanied their mothers to safety. At least 70% of all battered women seeking shelter have children who accompany them, and 17% of the women bring along three or more children (MacLeod, 1987). Shelter staff pointed out the fact that the most vulnerable clients they had were financially dependent battered women who were responsible for their children. In addition, the children presented themselves with a number of emotional and behavioral problems that required immediate attention. However, the times when the children needed their mothers the most as principal caretaker, the mothers were unavailable, as a result of their own overwhelming needs related to their victimization. Pizzey (1977) identified this concern, noting that battered women may become labeled as unfit mothers, and their children may experience the further disruption of being moved from a shelter to foster home placements.

ESTIMATED INCIDENCE OF CHILDREN WHO WITNESS VIOLENCE IN THE FAMILY

Current studies suggest that at least one in ten women are abused every year by the man with whom they live (MacLeod, 1987). Repeated, severe violence occurs in one in fourteen marriages (Dutton, 1988). Estimates have pointed to the fact that approximately 3 million to 4 million American households and 500,000 Canadian households live with this violence every year (MacLeod, 1987; Stark, Flitcraft, Zuckerman, Gray, & Frazier, 1981). The extremes of this violence are demonstrated by the fact that women in North America are more likely to be killed by their partners than by anyone else. The magnitude of the problem in terms of a known war is captured by statistics that indicate that the United States lost 39,000 soldiers in the line of duty during the Vietnam War while during the same time period (1967-1973) 17,500 American women and children were killed by members of their families (Grusznski, Brink, & Edleson, 1988). More women are abused by their husbands or boyfriends than are injured in car accidents, muggings, or rapes (Toufexis, 1987).

Straus and his colleagues (1980) have completed the most detailed study of violence in American families through 2,143 family interviews. This research, which pioneered the development of the Conflict Tactics Scale, discovered a wide variety of emotional and physical abuse in the family. Although Straus found a high incidence of husband abuse as well, subsequent researchers have noted that much of this behavior is in self-defense and may not cause the same degree of injuries and hospitalization (Dutton, 1988). From Straus's initial and more recent study of family violence, the type of actions and the frequency of their occurrence that children may observe are shown in Table 1.1.

Straus points out that children are often in the middle of this violence in a number of ways. Arguments about child-rearing practice and children's behavior are a major precipitating crisis that leads to violent episodes. Although children are not the cause of the violence, many children blame themselves for the violence because of the sequence of events and the family's inability to examine the real underlying factors. As stated by the authors,

> Even though there is little difference in the amount of conflict over money, sex, housekeeping, children, or social activities, a disagreement on one of these may still cause more trouble than a disagreement on another. Sex and money are widely believed to be the issues which cause the most trouble. But our data show that neither of these provoked the most violence. Rather, it is conflict over children which is most likely to lead a couple to blows. The more often a couple disagree about things concerning their children, the higher the

Table 1.1 Frequency of Husband to Wife Violence in Previous 12-Month Period

Category	*Rate Per 1000 Wives*	
	1980	*1988*
Threw something	28	28
Pushed, grabbed, shoved	107	93
Slapped	51	29
Kick, bit, or punched	24	15
Hit or tried to hit with something	22	17
Beat up	11	8
Threatened with a knife or gun	4	4
Used a knife or gun	3	2

SOURCE: Straus, M.A., Gelles, R.J., & Steinmetz, S. (1980). *Behind closed doors.* New York: Doubleday, Anchor Press; Gelles, R.J., & Straus, M.A. (1988). *Intimate violence.* New York: Simon and Schuster.

> rate of violence. In fact, two-thirds of the couples who said they always disagree over the children had at least one violent incident during the year of our survey! Children are a tremendous source of pride and satisfaction. Parents feel intensely about their children and their children's welfare, probably more intensely than about anything else in the family. It follows that when things go wrong with the children—as they inevitably do at some time or other—there are equal depths of despair, anguish, and conflict. (Straus et al., 1980, pp. 171-172)

Are children present during the violence? Carlson (1984) estimates (based on an average of two children in 55% of violent households) that at least 3.3 million children in the United States between the ages of 3 and 17 years are yearly at risk of exposure to parental violence. From our own clinical experience, many parents minimize or deny the presence of children during incidents of wife assault by suggesting that the children were asleep or playing outside. However, from interviews with children, we find that almost all can describe detailed accounts of violent behavior that their mother or father never realized they had witnessed (see also Rosenberg, 1984). Similarly, Bard (1970), in an evaluation of a police crisis intervention program in New York City, found that children were present in 41% of the "domestic disturbances" that led to a police intervention (an alarmingly high rate considering the likelihood that police become involved in a relatively small percentage of domestic assaults). A Toronto, Ontario, research project indicated that 68% of 2,910 wife assault cases had children present (Leighton, 1989). Finally, Sinclair (1985), based on her clinical experience, has suggested that if children are in a violent family 80% of them will witness an episode of wife assault. What they witness may range from a fleeting moment of abusive language to a homicide. Extreme events will stay with them for a lifetime and may be relived through subsequent court hearings (Bowker, Arbittel, & McFerron, 1988).

Many authors have also noted a significant overlap between wife assault and child abuse. There is reason to suspect that many children suffer from repeated exposure to violence, both as direct and as indirect victims. For example, retrospective accounts from women in shelters reveal that as many as 80% of the women recall witnessing their mother being assaulted by their father as well as being assaulted themselves (Gayford, 1975). In a community sample of battered women who were not residing in crisis shelters, almost one-third indicated that they had witnessed violence and had been abused themselves (Kincaid, 1982). Based on the histories and symptoms of battered women and their children in shelters, researchers estimate the extent of overlap between wife assault and child physical or sexual abuse to be approximately 30% to 40% (Hughes, 1982; Straus et al., 1980).

Children may find themselves at risk for witnessing violence during significant periods of the family's history. Even before they are born, some children face the dangers of family violence. Gelles (1975) and others have indicated that pregnancy can be a critical period related to wife assault, with very serious consequences for women and children. Moore (1979) also reported that wife battering was most likely to occur within a family as soon as children became family members. Her research led her to suggest that wife battering, like child abuse, was associated with the early years or the teen years. Infants and toddlers were seen to add a significant stressor for the family and to leave women in the most vulnerable position in regard to battering. Other authors also point to the beginning of adolescence as a critical time in marital adjustment and violence (Langley & Levy, 1977). In many instances, increased violence is precipitated by the very problems of adolescence (delinquency, running away) that may be associated with older children reacting to many years of witnessing their mother being assaulted by their father (Pizzey, 1977).

CHARACTERISTICS OF CHILDREN AND FAMILIES

Considerable research over the past decade has profiled battered women, their partners, and their children. Although consistent patterns of behavior have been described from observations of battered women and their families, what is often unclear is the extent to which certain personality and psychological factors precede or result from living with violence. Some of these descriptive factors are briefly discussed below.

Battered Women

Most studies of battered women involved those victims who sought refuge in a shelter after a serious incident of violence, which most likely represents a bias toward economic and social disadvantage. Yet, as recent studies have begun to examine a broader community sample of victims who had approached nonresidential services for legal and emotional counseling, researchers are discovering the existence of a wider range of psychological and social conditions among victims of all socioeconomic backgrounds than was previously acknowledged (Greaves, Heapy, & Wylie, 1988). Many of these specific stress-related disorders are discussed further in Chapter 3.

Many battered women not only are coping with the present violence but are also struggling with the trauma of their personal histories. A significant percentage of battered women have childhoods marked by witnessing violence themselves or being physically and sexually abused. The impact of their current victimization is undoubtedly magnified by these previous experiences (Hughes, 1982).

The Battered Woman's Syndrome (Walker, 1979) is now well accepted by most professionals working in the field as well as by many courts who try to understand victims' behavior. The syndrome is marked by a victim's increasing sense of helplessness and hopelessness about finding safety and terminating the violence. These feelings are reinforced by a sense of isolation and poor self-esteem, fostered by the batterer. Over time, victims can begin to deny and minimize the extent of the violence and underestimate the lethality of the situation for themselves and their children (Browne, 1987).

For the most part a victim's sense of isolation and being a prisoner in her own home is maintained by real economic and social factors that limit alternative solutions (Schechter & Gary, 1988). This victimization has direct implications for a mother's effectiveness as a parent because the vast majority are principal caretakers for their children. Battered women's role as parents is radically demeaned through their victimization, because the dysfunction and disorganization offers little nurturance, support, structure, or supervision for children. In extreme cases children may themselves be abused or neglected by the mothers they depend on (Bowker et al., 1988). As pointed out earlier, the children's misbehavior and special needs are at a peak when their mother's ability to respond to them is at a low point.

Men Who Batter

As outlined previously, a very common factor associated with men battering their partners is witnessing violence in their own families of origin. Interviews with batterers consistently point to childhood experiences of exposure to wife assault and, in many histories, direct physical abuse by their fathers as well (Dutton, 1988). Accordingly, violence is learned as the basis of power and control in the family.

Batterers' childhood experiences often come out after they have suffered the consequences of their own violence through police interventions or the loss of their families. Poignant examples of this experience were recently provided to us by Mark Holmes, a social worker with Catholic Family Services of Ottawa-Carlton (Ontario), who has been active in developing group counseling programs for abusive husbands in his region. As part of his intervention, men were asked to reflect on their childhood by writing a letter to their mothers and/or fathers. Examples of the responses he received follow:

> Batterer No. 1: To my Father: Dad, I wish when I was young that you would [have] showed more love and understanding. I did not want you to drink or to hit my mother. I really hated you for that. People have told me that you beat me when I was young, but I can't remember that. I remember the humiliation when we went out anywhere and you got drunk and would piss in your pants.
>
> When we moved out west you didn't realize the changes that made on me. I felt like an outsider at school, the gym teacher would not have me in his class because I was not good enough in sports. I was sexually abused.
>
> I tried to help the family by joining Al-Anon and leaving pamphlets around the house only to return to a empty fridge, arguments. I watched my mother have a depression, start drinking and going out with another man. I couldn't reproach her because I liked the other man. He was good to her and was not an alcoholic. These were the days I needed you most. Where were you? Today you're nothing but skin and bones. You still drink, and you hurt physically and emotionally. You repeat yourself. I visit you occasionally more out of a sense of duty.
>
> I do feel some love towards you, but I feel sorry and angry for the weaknesses I see in myself today.
>
> I live in the hope that I may be able to change my life and break this cycle of anger and resentment that I have been carrying all these years. I know your life was not easy, but you're 66 years old now and you had many chances to make a choice for better or worse.
>
> To my Mother: I have a mixture of love and hate towards you. I wish you had realized sooner the damage my father was doing to you and your family. When I ran away from home to grand-mother you got separated and left with me. You continued drinking and lost a good man along the way. The other men you brought to the house were repulsive (all alcoholics or worse). You tried your best; you completely transformed. You talked crazy, used to phone me at 3 in the morning or whenever and just yell things at me. When I was 20 and out of work I asked if you would take me in for a few months, and you said no because you were afraid me and my brother would really hurt ourselves. Maybe that was true at that time but it hurt like hell. Even to this day whenever there is aura of tension, I don't know when things will explode. At one stage or another I've tried to help all of you, but you all have chosen your own ways. I refuse to be intimidated anymore by what you think. I have my own life to take care of and that's going to take a lot of work. One last word to Dad; I really hated how you used to force Mommy to give you her hard-earned cheque so you could blow it on alcohol. Your drinking was more important than food, rent or anybody's feelings.

I have often asked the good Lord to forgive you (both father & mother & brothers) for what you have done to me emotionally and more important for the Lord to forgive me for the anger, hate and resentment that I bear towards you. I try hard and trust the Lord will give me that spirit of forgiveness I so desperately seek.

Batterer No. 2: Dear Mom: A lot has happened to me in the past year. I have really made a mess out of my life and marriage, but I am trying to get myself back to a state where I can accept what I am doing. I have done a lot of thinking about how I got to where I am now, and how growing up the way I did has affected me. I see so many of the things I didn't like about Dad in the way I act. So often I wish that Dad was never an alcoholic and that he could have been around to be a better father to us when we were growing up. I can remember always wishing he just wouldn't come home from work because I knew, no matter what, that there was going to be a fight. That's why we all tried to spend so much time away from the house when he was around. I was always afraid of what he was going to do, because we never knew. I'll always remember the day he ran you over with the truck because he was mad at me. We all thought he had killed you. Why was he always so drunk and angry, and why did you put up with it?

I know a lot of my attitude problem has to do with the way I saw Dad act and the way he treated you and us. I always said I would never be like he was, but I guess there are things that have stayed with me. At least I'm not an alcoholic, but I wonder now why I had to be so involved with drugs. I thought that it wasn't anything like being a drunk and that it was even helping me, but was I ever wrong. It would be nice if it was possible for him and I to sit down and talk without having to start shouting about everything and getting into an argument. And I wish that you and I could have been closer. We really don't know much about each other. Maybe that can change but I don't know if Dad can ever change. I still care a lot about both of you because you are my parents and you did help I guess as best as you could.

Batterer No. 3: Dear Dad: I find it very hard to deal with the way you have embarrassed/intimidated and abused me over the years. I don't understand how I can love you and hate you at the same time. It makes me very angry that you do not deal with things like normal families do. I am tired of being afraid of you.

Your abuse has only made we want to fight back at you now.

I am very afraid for myself because I believe I have become just like you.

Batterer No. 4: Dear Dad: I love and respect you very much. When I was young you wanted me to be tough. Well I am and I'm also a wife abuser. I wanted to be just like you and be the man of the house. I found as well as you

> [that] times have changed. Women wanted to be treated equal and I can't blame them. I'm not abusive to my kids as you were to me but I put them through hell. Well Dad, I forgive you for anything you might have done in my childhood. You did what you thought was right. Dad, this is my last chance for a family life. I screwed up lots before. Wish me well.
>
> Batterer No. 5: Dear Step Father: When you beat mom, me and the rest of the kids, I hated you. My hate lasted a long time, I wasn't sad or upset when you died. I think that I still have hate locked up inside of me, all caused by you. Why can't you just love us like we all wanted to love you?

Aside from retrospective accounts of batterers' childhood experiences, more recent studies have suggested that men who batter may lack the verbal skills required to negotiate nonviolent conflict resolution and have poor impulse control and a rigid style of demanding and controlling behaviors. Of particular significance as well is the idea that many violent episodes have no clear external antecedents or may be a misinterpretation of the partner's behavior (Dutton, 1988). For example, a woman's choice to obtain a part-time job or upgrade her education is interpreted to be an attempt to humiliate a husband by publicly suggesting he is unable to look after his dependent partner.

Batterers find ways to isolate their wives and children in order to decrease the likelihood of detection and assistance. In most families secrecy is an important value. Extreme jealousy can be apparent from the involvement of any "outsiders." Even a walk to the corner store is a threat to a husband who worries constantly that his wife may lose her prisoner status (Gelles, 1987). Violence is the means of maintaining fear in all family members. Children may be asked to watch their mother's victimization as a lesson in control and what may happen to them if they disobey their father (Finkelhor, Gelles, Hotaling, & Straus, 1983). Over time this experience is associated with the batterer's tone of voice and/or a facial expression and these cues alone can cause a high level of fear and intimidation.

Alcohol is present in almost half of all incidents of wife assault, although most researchers indicate a correlational rather than a causal relationship (Schechter & Gary, 1988). Alcohol abuse by the batterer obviously compounds the family's disorganization and increases the number of crises that require police intervention. The batterer and his victim usually minimize the violent behavior and focus on the alcohol as the root cause of any family problem (Pagelow, 1984). Continued alcohol abuse obviously leads to serious economic and social consequences for the family, which creates a greater need for the victim to look after the batterer. The children continue to cope with the violence in the context of further economic and social disadvantage.

The Children

Children's responses to witnessing their mother being assaulted by their father will vary according to their age, sex, stage of development, and role in the family. Many other factors will play a role, such as the extent and frequency of the violence, repeated separations and moves, economic and social disadvantage, and special needs that a child may have independent of this violence (e.g., significant learning disabilities). Although studies relating to children are reviewed in more detail in the next chapter, a descriptive overview of their adjustment difficulties is provided here.

Infants who are raised in an environment of wife abuse may suffer serious, unintended consequences. Their basic needs for attachment to their mother may be significantly disrupted. Routines around sleeping and feeding may become far from normal. A mother living in fear of her husband may be unable to handle the stressful demands of an infant. Clearly, an infant will recognize this distance and lack of availability of his or her principal caretaker (Hart & Brassard, 1987). Infants or young toddlers may also be injured in a violent episode by being "caught in the cross fire." They may accidentally be hit, pushed, or dropped during a violent outburst, or their mother may hold them for their own safety but discover that their father has no regard for their physical and emotional vulnerability.

Latency-age children look to their parents as significant role models. Boys and girls who witness violence quickly learn that violence is an appropriate way of resolving conflict in human relationships. Girls may learn that victimization is inevitable and no one can help change this pattern. Suffering in silence is reinforced. Children may attempt to practice what they have learned at home in the community through fights in the neighborhood or at school. Externalizing behavior problems will undermine their school adjustment and trigger consequences from the school system that aggravate the existing stressors in their home.

For latency-age children the consequences of exposure to wife assault may also lead to significant emotional difficulties. These children may live in shame in terms of the hidden violence and be embarrassed by the family secret. These feelings are often fluctuating with the idea that maybe someone will find out and rescue them (Davidson, 1978). The children's experience undermines their sense of self-esteem and the confidence they have in the future. They may have few opportunities to develop outside the family because of their father's domination and control, which isolates them and keeps them from extracurricular activities. These children may also experience guilt out of a sense that perhaps they could prevent the violence. If only they were "better" children, their father would not get so upset and be violent toward their mother. They are often confused by the violence and have a divided sense of loyalty in wanting to protect their mother, but still respecting and fearing their father's right to control their family.

Many children live with fear and anxiety, waiting for the next violent episode. They feel no safety in their own home yet are too young to seek out or even want an alternative. They may spend most of their hours in school distracted and inattentive to the academic tasks before them. At night they remain alert for the early warning signs of more violence. Little peace or security is available for these children.

Adolescence is a time when children first develop intimate relationships outside their families and can practice the sex role and communication patterns they have learned. For some youngsters it is the beginning of violence within their own relationships in dating and early courtship. For adolescent girls it is a crucial turning point in which they may start to accept threats and violence from boyfriends who control them through this behavior. As one study puts it, "What really gets me down [in the transition house] is seeing the daughters of women we sheltered and counseled 10 years ago coming to us as battered wives. Even when their mothers got their 'heads together' and got away from the violence, their daughters are repeating the pattern" (MacLeod, 1987, p. 33).

Many adolescents have lived with the violence in their families for many years, accompanied by physical and emotional abuse. One study of mothers in shelters reported that half of them had been battered for more than five years on a weekly basis and in some instances the battering was almost a daily occurrence (Layzer, Goodson, & deLange, 1985). In seeking their independence and relief from the family distress and violence, adolescents realize that there may be an escape. Although their mother may be a prisoner, they recognize that there may be some hope in trying to spend more time away from the home even if it means running away (Davidson, 1978). It is interesting to note that most interviews of runaway children and adolescents point to family conflict and exposure to violence as a major factor on the decision to run:

> With both wives and teenagers, independence is often an issue. For example, when wives and adolescents assert their autonomy and the authority figure reacts with anger, violence is always an implicit possibility, particularly in a

BATTERER	BATTERED MATE	CHILDREN
Batterers are found in all socioeconomic, educational, ethnic, racial and age groups	*Battered mates are found in all socioeconomic, educational, ethnic, racial and age groups*	*Children are found in all socioeconomic, educational, ethnic, racial and age groups*
. . . use psychological, verbal and physical abuse including sexual abuse.	. . . are psychologically, verbally and physically abused. Are frequently sexually abused.	. . . are psychologically abused and may be verbally, physically and sexually abused.
. . . engage in excessive minimization and denial.	. . . engage in excessive minimization and denial.	. . . engage in excessive minimization and denial.
The batterer is characterized by	**The battered mate is characterized by**	**Children in violent homes are characterized by**
. . . poor impulse control—limited tolerance for frustration, explosive temper—rage. Constantly demonstrating, but often successfully masking anger.	. . . long-suffering, martyrlike endurance of frustration, passive acceptance, internalizing anger.	. . . a combination of limited tolerance for frustration, poor impulse control and martyrlike long-suffering—they externalize/internalize anger.
. . . stress disorders and psychosomatic complaints; sophistication of symptoms and success at masking dysfunction vary with social and educational levels.	. . . stress disorders and psychosomatic complaints.	. . . sadness, depression, stress disorders and psychosomatic complaints; absences from school, pre-delinquent and delinquent behaviour.
. . . emotional dependency—subject to secret depressions known only to family.	. . . economic and emotional dependency; subject to depression, high risk for secret drugs and alcohol, home accidents.	. . . economic and emotional dependency, high risk for alcohol/drugs, sexual acting out, running away, isolation, loneliness and fear.
. . . limited capacity for delayed reinforcement—very "now" oriented.	. . . unlimited patience for discovery of "magic combination" in solving marital and abusive problems—"travels miles" on bits of reinforcement.	. . . combination of poor impulse control and continual hopefulness that situation will improve.
. . . insatiable ego needs and qualities of childlike narcissism (not generally detectable to people outside family group).	. . . being unsure of own ego needs, defining self in terms of partner, children, family, job.	. . . very shaky definition of self—grappling with childlike responses of parents for modeling; poor definition of self and/or defines self in parenting role (role reversal)
. . . low self-esteem; perceived unachieved ideals and goals for self, disappointment in career, even if successful by others' standards.	. . . low self-esteem, continued faith and hope that battering mate will get "lucky" break.	. . . low self-esteem, seeing self and siblings with few options or expectations to succeed.
. . . qualities which suggest great potential for change and improvement; i.e., makes frequent "promises" for the future.	. . . unrealistic hope that change is imminent, belief in "promises."	. . . mixture of hope/depression that there is no way out; peer group can be most important contact, if available.
. . . perception of self as having poor social skills; describing relationship with mate as closest he has ever known; remaining in contact with his own family.	. . . gradually increasing social isolation including loss of contact with own family and friends.	. . . increased social isolation, increased peer isolation *or* complete identification with peers. Poor social skills.
. . . accusations against mate, jealousy, voicing great fear of abandonment or "being cheated on," possessive, controlling, hovering.	. . . inability to convince partner of loyalty, futilely guarding against accusations of "seductive" behavior toward others; compliant, helpless and powerless.	. . . bargaining behavior with parents; attempts to prove self; compliant, but may run away. Feelings of powerlessness.

Figure 1.1 Behavioral Characteristics of Domestic Violence

SOURCE: Vicki D. Boyd & Karil S. Klingbeil. Revised January 1984. Seattle, Washington. Used by permission.

BATTERER	BATTERED MATE	CHILDREN
The batterer is characterized by	**The battered mate is characterized by**	**Children in violent homes are characterized by**
. . . fearfulness that partner and/or children will abandon, fear of being alone.	. . . constant fear, which gradually becomes cumulative and oppressive with time.	. . . constant fear and terror for their life as well as parents; confusion and insecurity.
. . . containment of mate and employment of espionage tactics against her (e.g., checks mileage/times errands); cleverness depends on level of sophistication.	. . . helplessly allowing containment or confinement/restriction by mate mistakenly interpreted as sign that partner "cares."	. . . increasing deceptiveness: lying, excuses for outings, stealing, cheating.
. . . violating others' personal boundaries; accepts no blame for failure (marital, familial, or occupational) or for violent acts.	. . . gradually losing sight of personal boundaries for self and children (unable to assess danger accurately), accepts all blame.	. . . poor definition of personal boundaries, violation of others personal boundaries, accepting blame or projecting blame.
. . . belief that forcible behavior is aimed at securing the family nucleus ("for the good of the family").	. . . belief that transient acceptance of violent behavior will ultimately lead to long term resolution of family problems.	. . . little or no understanding of the dynamics of violence; often assumes violence to be the norm.
. . . absence of guilt on an emotional level even after intellectual recognition.	. . . emotional acceptance of guilt for mate's behavior, thinking mate "can't help it," considering own behavior as provocative.	. . . self-blame (depending on age) for family feuding, separations, divorce, & internal conflicts.
. . . generational history of abuse.	. . . generational history of witnessing abuse in family and/or being abused.	. . . continuation of abuse pattern in adult life.
. . . frequently participating in pecking order battering.	. . . occasionally participating in pecking order battering.	. . . frequently participating in pecking order battering (maim or kill animals, batter siblings); oftimes batters parents in later years.
. . . assaultive skills which improve with age and experience (increase in danger potential and lethality risks to family members over time).	. . . "creative" behavior which either diverts or precipitates mate's violence; but level of carelessness increases (judgment of lethality potential deteriorates) over time.	. . . poor problem-solving skills: may use violence as problem-solving technique in school, with peers, with family (appears as early as preschool) demonstrates aggression *or* passivity.
. . . demanding and oftentimes assaultive role in sexual activities: sometimes punishes w/abstinence, at times experiences impotence.	. . . poor sexual self-image, assuming that role is total acceptance of partner's sexual behavior. Attempts at abstinence result in further abuse.	. . . poor sexual image, uncertainty about appropriate behavior, confused model identification, immaturity in peer relationships.
. . . increasingly assaultive behavior when mate is pregnant – pregnancy often marks the first assault.	. . . being at high risk for assaults during pregnancy.	. . . being at higher risk for assaults (either as witnesses or victims) during mother's pregnancy.
. . . exerting control over mate by threatening homicide and/or suicide . . . often attempts one or both when partners separate – known to complete either or both.	. . . frequent contemplation of suicide – history of minor attempts, occasionally completing suicide or becoming a homicide victim, frequently wishing partner dead. Occasionally completes homicide in self-defense.	. . . heightened suicide risks and attempts – increased thoughts of suicide and/or murdering parents, prone to negligence and carelessness.
. . . frequently using children as "pawns" and exerting power and control through custody issues . . . may kidnap children or hold them hostage.	. . . feeling powerless in custody issues, living in fear children will be "kidnapped," struggling to maintain rights of children.	. . . feeling used and powerless in all decisions (age specific) regarding custody issues.

Figure 1.1 Continued.

> culture such as our own that condones violence as an expression of concern and as a disciplinary tactic. The independence of the previously submissive, intimate loved one particularly threatens a personality that needs absolute compliance from its dependents in order to confirm its own validity. Many authority figures simply lose control of their impulses when a challenge becomes unbearable. Teenagers are notorious for their expertise at provoking anger in their parents. Like wives, they are thus more capable of precipitating their own abuse. This does not mean that wives and teenagers are really to blame, or that they are responsible for their own abuse. However, it means that they are integrally involved in a system of relating that does not work. They will need to learn new ways to respond, as will the aggressors. Without justifying abuse, we must note that the perpetrator is often a victim of circumstances. (Garbarino & Gillian, 1980, p. 114)

Adolescents may confront their mothers with the fact that they cannot live with violence any more. Sadly, the mother was often staying with her husband to provide the children with the "stability" of a male-dominated household (Davidson, 1978). Some adolescents begin to act out their anger and frustration in more dramatic ways that result in delinquencies and the interventions of the juvenile justice system (Grusznski et al., 1988). Some adolescent boys handle their frustration with the behavior that has been most clearly modeled for them by assaulting their mother or siblings (Straus et al., 1980, p. 104):

> Beaten wives we interviewed told us that their children began threatening them after seeing their fathers become violent. A child who sees his mother hit by his father comes to view hitting as the thing to do – a means of getting what he wants. Some mothers of young children report that when they refuse to give their child candy or cookies, the child will indignantly retort: "You better give me some candy, or I'll get Daddy to hit you!" Later on, the child takes matters into his own hands. Our survey uncovered many women battered by both their husbands and their teen-age children.

While witnessing violence may lead some adolescents to run away or become involved in delinquent behavior, other adolescents may take on additional responsibilities to keep the peace and provide safety for their families. Older youngsters, especially girls and those with younger siblings, may take over parenting responsibility for most members of the household. They protect younger siblings during violent episodes and offer support or reassurance in the aftermath of the violent behavior. These adolescents may feel they cannot leave home because they have to protect their mother or find ways to calm their father's angry outbursts. Obviously these responsibilities are a heavy burden for young men and women who often carry this role into their early adult years.

Some of the characteristics of battered women, their husbands, and child witnesses to this violence have been outlined above. These characteristics are all interrelated. Obviously, a husband's domination and control through aggressive acts will create a number of physical and emotional adjustment problems for his wife. Children will be affected by what behaviors are modeled, by the trauma they are experiencing, and by the distress of their parents. The cruel irony for these children is that the very adults on whom they depend for safety and nurturance can offer neither safety nor nurturance (Van der Kolk, 1987).

Klingbeil and Boyd (1984), in their efforts to educate medical professionals in hospital emergency rooms, offered an excellent framework for understanding battered women and their families by charting the interrelationships among behavioral characteristics of family members. Figure 1.1 provides a summary of behavioral characteristics of batterers and the resulting symptoms of their victims. This figure is an important reminder that behavioral characteristics do not exist in isolation from the violence in these families.

SUMMARY

This chapter has placed the study of children of battered women into a historical perspective by examining the literature's initial references to this population. Through the many tragic case histories of children who witness violence as well as the retrospective accounts of battered women and their partners, a terrifying portrait of fear and chaos emerges. Equally alarming are some of the estimates of the scope of the problem, which suggest that several million children in North America witness their mothers being abused. The potential consequences for these children in terms of their emotional and social development was outlined in this chapter. In the next two chapters the impact of witnessing violence will be examined in greater detail and a theoretical framework will be explored to better understand how children are affected by this violence.

2

FAMILY VIOLENCE AND CHILDREN'S DEVELOPMENT

The diversity of problems exhibited by children of battered women requires considerable knowledge of how children's development can be affected by negative family experiences. Based on studies of child development in normal families, it is believed that a child's sense of self and his or her development of emotional expression stem from important early experiences involving significant members of the family. Because the nature of family violence is such that it represents a highly emotion-charged experience (in which the child is typically not an active participant), it is critical to ask the question as to whether a child's social and emotional functioning can be altered significantly by exposure to such events. If such a suspected negative influence can indeed be confirmed, it is necessary to ask whether there is a stable link between the child's disrupted development and his or her expression of psychological adjustment problems later on. In pursuit of these areas of understanding, this chapter discusses two interrelated research themes: the first addresses the manner in which young children develop behavioral adjustment problems over time and the second looks at the influence of the emotions of others on children's development. Findings from recent empirical studies of children of battered women are interspersed throughout the discussions of both of these issues.

The lack of attention afforded to the understanding of family violence and children's development is evident from the conspicuous absence of this topic throughout the psychological literature until very recently. A search of major child development textbooks over the past five decades reveals that the issue of family violence has only surfaced in the last 15 years or so. Prior to 1960, major texts either made no mention at all of parental conflict or violence (e.g., Gessell, 1943; Thorpe, 1946) or brought up the issue only in a tangential manner by referring vaguely to parental friction (e.g., "interparental friction may have an adverse influence on children's adjustments," Mussen & Conger, 1956, p. 257) or to family pathology, which was often defined as consisting of the death of one or both parents, illegitimate children, divorce, and economic deprivation (e.g., Stone & Church, 1957, pp. 378-381). The classic theoretical book by Eric Erikson (1963) *Childhood and Society* likewise made no mention of family violence, the witnessing of wife abuse, or similar traumatic events imposed on children by family members (other than certain developmental milestones that were potentially traumatic, according to psychoanalytic theory).

The developing emphasis on divorce and separation was reflected by the second edition of some of these major texts in the 1960s, as was the issue of physical child abuse (e.g., Mussen, Conger, & Kagan, 1983; Stone & Church, 1988), but again there was no mention of spousal violence and its possible impact on child development. *Violence* began to appear in the indexes of these texts in the 1970s, yet the term was referring only to the behavior of the children, not the parents! For example, Stone and Church's third edition (1973) discussed violence in relation to juvenile delinquency, as did the fourth edition of Mussen, Conger, and Kagan (1974). These latter texts came to highlight the growing awareness that delinquency was associated with parents who were hostile and who lacked the ability to generate family cohesiveness and shared goals. These texts also began to note that, even among nondelinquent populations of children, those whose parents were frequently characterized as rejecting and neglectful were more likely than other children to engage in aggressive, acting-out behavior.

It was not until this past decade that family discord and spousal violence reached center stage as possible predeterminants of developmental psychopathology. For example, Shaffer (1988, p. 256) noted, "There is now ample evidence that the emotional climate of the home can and often does influence children's behavior." In addition, books written specifically on the topic of childhood violence and trauma began to underscore the relationship and common occurrence of these events. In commenting on the startling prevalence of such events in the lives of children, Carlson (1984) suggested that children at various stages of development are differentially able to understand and cope with what is happening between their parents as a function of their cognitive abilities and resources for adaptation. In parallel, longitudinal studies—originally designed to explore the development of delinquency in children—emerged with the conclusion that ongoing parental conflict and violence in childhood were significantly predictive of serious personal crimes in adulthood (e.g., assault, attempted rape, rape, attempted murder, kidnapping, and murder) and less predictive of serious adult property crimes (see, for example, McCord, 1983; Standing Senate Committee on Health, Welfare, and Science, 1980). In his recent book on psychological trauma, Van der Kolk (1987, p. 14) noted that the emotional development of children "is intimately connected with the safety and nurturance provided by their environment." Furthermore, he stressed that the developmental age of the victim and stage of the relationship with the offender must be taken into account when determining whether and in what manner a particular incident may or may not be traumatic to the child.

EARLY DESCRIPTIONS OF CHILDREN RESIDING IN SHELTERS FOR BATTERED WOMEN

In addition to being mentioned in the literature on delinquency, the link between family violence and children's development was established initially by published descriptions of the observed adjustment problems of children who came to shelters with their mothers to escape violent partners. These accounts alerted others to the stress-related disorders that a significant percentage of these children were displaying, including physical health problems, acting-out problems, and a wide range of disorders reflecting low self-concept, fear and anxiety, and social isolation. An overview is provided below of the health and behavior problems of these children that first emerged from shelter staff descriptions, followed by the views and opinions offered by experienced child-care workers and clinicians as to the impact of these events on the children's lives. These views form the basis for the subsequent in-depth analysis of the developmental issues and adjustment disorders that are currently being investigated with this population of children.

Health and Behavior Problems

Layzer at al. (1985) reported on their findings from six shelter-based research projects funded in 1981 by the National Center for Child Abuse and Neglect. Their data provide a rich source of information concerning the demographic and psychological profiles of these children and their mothers. The majority of mothers who sought help from one of the shelters brought their children with them (less than one-fifth left one or more children at home, usually adolescents). The most frequent age range of children at the shelters was preschool, with an equal division of very young (infants and toddlers) and school-aged children. Overall, the researchers noted very few physical characteristics of the children that distinguished them from children in demographically similar, but nonviolent, families. The vast majority were the mothers' natural children, with 17% being stepchildren of the batterer.

Although few children had chronic mental or physical health problems, many exhibited acute health and behavior problems in the shelter that most likely were related to their environment (as described below), with those children who were known to have been abused or neglected in addition to witnessing family violence having the highest incidence of problems. Based on caseworker assessments, over half of the infants had health problems, including weight and eating problems, sleeping problems, and lack of responsiveness to adults. Among the children over 18 months of age, nearly 70% exhibited mood-related disorders, including anxiousness, crying, and sadness. This age group of children was also observed to have problems interacting with peers or adults (40%), and one-third displayed health and sleep disturbances.

Hughes (1982) expressed similar observations of children residing at shelters for battered women. She described the vast majority of the children as being "emotionally needy," although how they expressed their needs differed greatly. Younger children, especially boys, were likely to act out, become disobedient, and behave defiantly and destructively in the shelter. Young girls in the shelters, on the other hand, were described as being withdrawn, clingy, and dependent. Adolescents presented an even more contrasting picture, often being resistant to the change of residence and preferring instead to remain at the homes of friends. Hughes (1982) also noted that many of the latency-aged boys (aged 6-11 years) strongly identified with their fathers, often expressing more ambivalence regarding their feelings for their fathers than did other age and sex groupings of children. These boys seemed to miss their fathers more than did their sisters, which the researcher suspected could produce intense feelings of conflict in these boys—they missed their father, yet they knew (at some level) that his behavior was inappropriate.

Shelter Staff Observations and Opinions of Children's Experiences and Adjustment

McKay (1981) asked staff in transition houses to indicate what they perceived to be the most important factors influencing the possibility of lasting adverse effects on children's development from witnessing wife abuse. Of the 90 staff members responding to her survey, 69% viewed psychological threats to family members as being the most important pathogenic factor, followed by the type of physical force used (43%), the child's disrupted routine (41%), and the severity of the force (37%). All staff agreed that children's exposure to wife assault would affect their development, either greatly or significantly. As well, 55 houses reported on their observations of the prevalence of different behavior disorders, including emotional (62%), conduct (51%), wetting and soiling (17%), facial tics (14%), and developmental disorders (22%). Staff estimated that only 14% of the children who came to the shelter showed little or no evidence of one or more of these adjustment disorders. Interestingly, 80% of the staff also noted clear sex differences in the expression of children's distress, describing the differences in terms of males being more aggressive and females being more passive.

Another informative and detailed account of the appearance and adjustment of children as they entered a shelter for the first time was reported by Sopp-Gilson (1980). Similar to other accounts, her findings show that children often exhibit above-average stress-related physical and emotional symptoms while at the shelter. They often appear unsettled and anxious, most likely because they now have to deal with the additional stress of moving away from home. This readjustment entails a separation from school and friends, fathers, toys, pets, and their most familiar objects and routine. She describes the children as being torn between feeling relieved that they are not at home and being terrified about not being there. This conundrum, it is believed, leads to children placing heavy pressure on their mothers to go home (a finding that was especially pertinent to school-aged children). Sopp-Gilson further noticed that, once children make it through the first 24 hours and past the immediate risk of feared consequences, they may go through a period of relief in which they seem to enjoy receiving the attention of staff and participating in the available activities. This attention is often in true contrast to the isolated family life they knew. Following this "setting in" period, an interesting pattern ensues, particularly among the younger boys, she notes. They begin to mimic male role models by becoming aggressive toward mothers, female staff, and peers. Consequently, mothers are faced with the difficulty of establishing behavioral control over their children under urgent circumstances. The children rebel to the limits set by mother and staff, which often leads to yelling, screaming, threatening, and hitting. Similar to other descriptions, this researcher's findings also describe the behavior of the girls in the shelter as being in sharp contrast to that of the boys, noting their quiet, withdrawn, and submissive style, as if girls were "trying hard not to be noticed."

Most descriptions of children in shelters for battered women also depict the scenes that these children have witnessed—such as their mothers being beaten, thrown into walls, pushed through windows, and having their eyes blackened and teeth knocked out—while emphasizing how the children receive an education in the effects of violence and fear. They have often lived through years of brutality, which becomes so much a part of their home lives that they have little appreciation of what "normal" should be. An interview with a 10-year-old shelter resident (cited in Sopp-Gilson, 1980, p. 3) illustrates this point:

> He told me of one Christmas dinner at his home when he and his mother and sister were seated around the table and everything all set and the turkey waiting to be carved. Their father, irritated about something, came into the room. He picked up the potato masher and pulverized the turkey. The boy said that when he and his sister talked about it later, they called it "the year the turkey got killed twice." When he finished telling me the story, he was looking at me with a strange look in his eyes. I asked what the look was about and he said, "Do you think that is weird?" He really was not sure whether that was normal behavior.

Based on these early observations by shelter staff, several research efforts have been undertaken to develop an understanding of the two major dimensions of childhood psychopathology that are often noted in descriptive accounts, that is, adjustment problems expressed as internalized symptoms (e.g., sadness, withdrawal, somatic complaints, fear, and anxiety) and problems expressed as externalizing symptoms (e.g., aggression, cruelty to animals, disobedience, destructiveness). Recent attention has also focused on related factors that are foundations of normal child development, such as social competence and school performance. These efforts have attempted to surmount the methodological problems that are inherent in the study of personal violence, such as the provision of a precise definition of what the children have experienced, measures of child adjustment derived from multiple and valid sources, adequate comparison groups, follow-up observations, and statistically aided interpretations of the impact of wife abuse on specific areas of children's development. The highlights of these empirical studies are presented in the next two sections, corresponding to (a) children's behavioral adjustment and (b) children's cognitive and emotional adjustment. Each section is introduced with relevant literature on normal child development to assist in understanding what implications these findings have to children's ongoing development.

THE BEHAVIORAL ADJUSTMENT OF CHILDREN OF BATTERED WOMEN

Theory Relating to Children's Abnormal Behavioral Development

Knowledge of the factors influencing children's behavioral adjustment has grown considerably in recent decades, and much of this information is pertinent to an understanding of the behavioral problems described among samples of children in shelters for battered women. First and foremost, prominent developmental theories stress the crucial role of the caregiver in setting the stage for the children's ongoing development. For example, theories of attachment (e.g., Bowlby, 1973; Sroufe & Fleeson, 1986) note that the early parent-child relationship sets the stage for the child's future development of relationships. If this early relationship is characterized by trust, reciprocity, consistency, and child-centered nurturing activities, the child's propensity to develop positive, desirable relations with peers and other adults is considered to be greatly enhanced. Alternatively, an early parent-child relationship marked by fear, inconsistency, and unmet physical and psychological needs is associated with poor formation of peer relationships and a higher frequency of behavioral and emotional disorders (e.g., Brassard et al., 1987).

In a similar vein, social-learning theorists studying family pathology (e.g., Dumas & Wahler, 1985; Patterson, 1986) raise as a central assumption the formation of a parent-child relationship that is built upon consistent parental responses to the child's prosocial and undesirable behavior, such as praising the child's attempts at compliance and effectively punishing the child's coercive, disruptive style of interacting. This process of effective child rearing merits some preliminary discussion in order to place the problems seen among children of battered women in a conceptual and developmental perspective.

The Role of the Caregiver

The work of Patterson and his colleagues (Patterson, 1986; Patterson, DeBarysche, & Ramsey, 1989) illustrates the crucial role of the caregiver in children's development of conduct disorders from a social-interactional (social-learning) model of family dynamics. Their central thesis, derived from repeated investigations of the interactions between members of families having a conduct-disordered child, is that these parents fail to punish everyday problem behaviors effectively and, simultaneously, train the child to engage in coercive interactions. The child's coercive, disruptive behavior results from ineffective attempts on the part of the parent to punish (decrease) the behavior, and in turn such behavior provides an arena in which the parent learns to escape in order to avoid the child's torment. Such escape-conditioning of the parent becomes (negatively) reinforced, because the child succeeds in getting his way and the parent avoids the aggravation of attempting to control the child. Key variables in this model include an unskilled parent and a difficult child and/or the presence of stressors or substance abuse among the parents, which serves to diminish their already limited skills (Patterson et al., 1989).

Attachment theorists also place heavy emphasis on the caregiver's interactive style with the child, which has relevance for explaining children's adaptation to violence. In studying the development of children's social relationships, developmentalists note that social relationships also have developmental significance and can be traced back to the interaction between caregiver and child (Hartup, 1989). The child's relationship development is a reciprocal process, involving much correcting on the part of both child and parent. From this early relationship, the child learns how to form relationships with others. In line with the work of Patterson (1986) and Patterson et al. (1989), aggressive and antisocial behavior patterns first arise in early family coercive interactions. The children are usually difficult to socialize, and the parents are inept socialization agents. The course of adjustment problems, accordingly, does not begin later on in childhood with associates who are themselves deviant; rather, such problems represent the final stage of a process that begins with poor relationship development and social failure (Hartup, 1989).

Behavior Problems Among Child Witnesses to Family Violence

Children's responses to observing violence between parents vary considerably, although the range of behavior problems reported by researchers and practitioners is remarkably congruent. No "typical reactions" to family violence seem to emerge, which is not surprising given the understanding that children's reactions represent their attempts to cope with extremely frightening and unpredictable events. Similar to the reactions of children who have been physically abused (Wolfe, Zak, Wilson, & Jaffe, 1986), the reactions of children who chronically witness family violence may include disruptions of normal developmental patterns that result in disturbed patterns of cognitive, emotional, and/or behavioral adjustment.

Despite the extreme diversity of reactions children may develop after exposure to recurring violence and stress, patterns and subgroups of children can be tentatively identified based on critical developmental and situational factors. Several identified factors that appear to influence the adjustment of children residing in shelters include their age and gender, the amount of violence they have witnessed, whether they were a victim as well as a bystander during family conflict, and the stability/severity of their mothers' mental health functioning over time (Hughes, 1986). These important influences will be considered throughout the following discussion of findings regarding the adjustment of children from violent homes.

Developmental Differences in Children's Adjustment

Children at various stages of development are differentially able to understand and cope with what is happening between their parents as a function of their cognitive abilities and adaptation skills. Based on clinical observation of children in shelters, Davidson (1978) and Alessi and Hearn (1984) have described the primary characteristics of different age groups of children. Infants who witness violence are often characterized by poor health, poor sleeping habits, and excessive screaming (all of which may contribute to further violence toward their mother). Among preschoolers, these researchers found signs of terror, as evidenced by the children's yelling, irritable behavior, hiding, shaking, and stuttering. Moreover, Hughes (1986) consistently found that preschoolers in shelters both are rated as and report themselves to be more distressed than is the case for older children. Younger children also appear to be more likely to experience somatic complaints and to regress to earlier stages of functioning. Initially sympathetic to their mothers' plight, these children sometimes replace this sympathy with anger and overt hostility as they mature (Hilberman & Munson, 1978).

For older children and adolescents, violence at home usually becomes more commonplace, yet children in this age group are often very guarded and secretive about the family situation and often deny it. Adolescents from violent families may use aggression as a predominant form of problem solving, may project blame onto others, and may exhibit a high degree of anxiety (e.g., bite nails, pull hair, somatize feelings; Alessi & Hearn, 1984; Davidson, 1978). Adolescents may become manipulators of the family system, not allowing mother to leave and disrupt the accustomed routine. Mother's suffering is part of the daily routine, and teens may depersonalize her and blame her for the family problems. Sadly, both boys and girls have been known to participate in the beating of their mother after having witnessed such behavior over many years. Running away is also common among this older age group, especially among males, and it is not uncommon for an older child to side with one parent (it was discovered by Straus et al., 1980, that those children who side with their father are more likely to behave violently toward their mother at some point in time). It is not surprising that ambivalent feelings toward either or both parents develop as a result of their juxtaposition in the family.

Gender-Related Differences in Children's Adjustment

By school age, gender-related differences in children's reactions to chronic family violence also begin to emerge. As previously noted, males are frequently described as being disruptive, acting aggressively toward objects and people, and throwing severe temper tantrums (Rosenbaum & O'Leary, 1981; Wolfe, Jaffe, Wilson, & Zak, 1985; Wolfe et al., 1986). In contrast, females are reported to have an increasing assortment of somatic complaints and are more likely to display withdrawn, passive, clinging, and dependent behavior (e.g., Hughes, 1986). As they get older, adolescent girls may develop an extreme distrust of men and express negative attitudes about marriage. As girls begin to date, they are more likely to be victims of physical violence from boyfriends, seeing such behavior as inevitable or an indicator of love.

One study to date, however, points to a possible interaction between the amount of violence the child has witnessed and the type of behavioral adjustment exhibited by males and females. Rosenberg (1984) discovered that, when there was a relatively lower occurrence of parental violence, boys selected aggressive coping strategies whereas girls reacted passively. Alternatively, when there was a higher occurrence of violence, girls chose aggressive methods for solving problems and boys became more passive. Although the mechanisms responsible for influencing the child's behavioral outcome are poorly understood, Rosenberg (1984) suspects that the child's predominant method of problem solving in interpersonal situations (a gender-related characteristic) becomes exaggerated following exposure to parental violence. Under more extreme conditions of exposure, however, children may attempt to escape or avoid the problem situations, or draw attention away from the parents and to themselves by resorting to more unusual and dramatic coping responses.

In sum, both clinical case descriptions and empirical studies indicate that children of all ages who have witnessed conjugal violence exhibit elevated behavior problems at home and in other settings (Fantuzzo & Lindquist, 1989). Other than developmental and gender differences, however, studies to date have not revealed the mechanisms by which some children act out more than others. The plight of children who witness wife battering, and the atmosphere that breeds their adjustment difficulties, is captured by the following description by Walker (1979, p. 46):

> Children who live in a battering relationship experience the most insidious form of child abuse. Whether or not they are physically abused by either parent is less important than the psychological scars they bear from watching their fathers beat their mothers. They learn to become part of a dishonest conspiracy of silence. They learn to lie to prevent inappropriate behavior, and they learn to suspend fulfillment of their needs rather than risk another confrontation. They do extend a lot of energy avoiding problems. They live in a world of make-believe.

COGNITIVE AND EMOTIONAL ADJUSTMENT OF CHILDREN OF BATTERED WOMEN

Although the behavioral adjustment problems of children from violent homes often are the most disruptive and disturbing characteristics of these children (i.e., such behavioral disturbances often are associated with child management problems, school problems, and lack of positive peer relations), practitioners and researchers have also noted a high incidence of less visible signs of developmental disturbances among this population of children and adolescents. Children in shelters, for example, are frequently described as being withdrawn, fearful, distraught, and prone to misinterpret the intentions of others.

A child's psychological adjustment includes aspects of internal functioning that do not lend themselves readily to specific observation and understanding, yet many reliable inferences can be drawn as to the relationship between observed behavioral expression (e.g., fearfulness) and the child's cognitive and emotional "processing" of information that precedes such an expression. As a prelude to the presentation of findings regarding the emotional and cognitive adjustment of children of battered women, the next subsection describes recent investigations of how children learn from the emotional expressions of others. The role of emotions in child development is discussed, as are recent studies exploring how adult conflict influences this role. The manner in which children attribute responsibility for adult anger is also explored via several innovative studies. These findings, based on different series of laboratory studies involving normal children, provide a framework for an understanding of the emotional and cognitive reactions of children from violent homes.

Developmental Theorists' Views of the Role of Emotions

Researchers are discovering a wealth of information relating to the role of emotion in children's lives, which may hold some of the key to an understanding of the manner in which exposure to wife abuse affects children's adjustment. In pursuing a better understanding of emotions, developmental theorists have applied a "functionalist perspective" of human emotions to the study of emotional development in infants and children. This perspective explains how young children learn from the emotional expressions of others as a result of the adaptive, functional nature of emotional reactions (Bretherton, Fritz, Zahn-Waxler, & Ridgeway, 1986). According to this view, emotions serve important functions that maintain their evolutionary status. These functions include adaptive, survival-promoting processes, such as an infant's fear of heights or strangers. Emotions also serve as important internal monitoring and guidance systems that are designed to appraise events as being beneficial or dangerous and to provide motivation for action. In a similar fashion, emotions serve interpersonal regulatory functions as well. A person may gain access to another's emotional state by reading facial, gestural, postural, and vocal cues. This latter function permits "social referencing," a process whereby an inexperienced person (e.g., a young child) may rely on a more experienced person's (e.g., an adult's) affective interpretation of an event (Bretherton et al., 1986).

Developmental evidence for this functionalist perspective of emotions among normal children has accumulated in recent years. For example, when a young infant is presented with a novel object, he or she looks for cues in the mother in order to recognize her emotion, which may convey information as to the pleasantness/unpleasantness of the unfamiliar object (Feinman, 1982). By age 2, children are also capable of making references to emotions in others. Based on naturalistic observations, Radke-Yarrow and Zahn-Waxler (unpublished, cited in Bretherton et al., 1986) found that 87% of their 2-year-old sample were making statements of verbal sympathy, reassurance, or concern for others. Most relevant to the present topic were the findings of children's comments in reaction to parental quarrels, indicating their recognition of the conflict and their attempts to offer help or criticism (e.g., statements such as "No not angry. Not nice.")

Children are also constantly gaining in their ability to contemplate emotion-related situations and offer explanations as to causes and consequences. For example, when presented with pictures in which the protagonist's facial expression does not match the situational cues (e.g., a happy adult face looking at a broken window and a child with a bat), preschoolers tend to go with the expression, whereas elementary-school-aged children tend to rely more on the situational cues (the window and bat) for their judgment of emotion. Even when the younger ones cannot provide a plausible explanation for the adult's expressed emotion, they still tend to go with the expression rather than the situational cues (Gnepp, 1983).

In short, developmental evidence suggests that children begin to learn the importance of emotions for communication and regulation early in the first year of life. By the second year, they are beginning to develop rudimentary attempts to attribute causes to emotional expressions ("He's sad, ice cream gone. She's scared, big dog."). Of particular interest to our current application is the finding that children look to the emotional expressions and cues of their caregivers to provide them with the information needed to formulate a basic understanding of "what's going on." In the absence of congruence between the parent's expressed emotion and the situational cues, young children tend to interpret a novel situation by reliance on facial/visual cues of emotion.

These findings have considerable significance for children's exposure to family violence. Such a scenario represents an arousing, emotion-laden situation in which the child's preconceived notion of his or her parent(s) is challenged by conflicting new information—parents who "care" for one another are now engaging in highly fearful, threatening behavior. The child looks for an explanation of how to respond and sees it in the faces of his or her parents: fear, apprehension, and anger. Similarly, the older child looks for explanations for the parents' behavior and utilizes the additional information provided by verbal cues (e.g., name calling, tone of voice), gestures, facial expressions, and so on. Moreover, as revealed by naturalistic studies, not only do parents contribute to the emotional expression of children, but children also may try to persuade their parents to tone down strong negative affect expressions. Such attempts on the part of children and youth are ill-fated when wife abuse occurs and can in fact have the opposite effect of elevating the emotion and the violence. These developmental issues will continue to be pursued vis-à-vis parental anger and violence in the following sections.

ADULT CONFLICT AND CHILDREN'S COPING REACTIONS: A LESSON TO LEARN

Much of the child development literature has focused on children's *direct* social and affective interactions with others, such as the development of attachment and social relationships, which require the child's active involvement and participation. However, it is also possible that children are affected by events that occur in their presence even though they do not participate. This possibility is the core issue in the study of children of battered woman, and it merits careful investigation.

The information on children's emotional development noted above indicates that children are quite sensitive to others' anger, yet until recently little direct information was available pertaining to the manner in which such sensitivity may be expressed by the child in the immediate and long term. At the U.S. National Institute of Mental Health (NIMH) Child Development Laboratory, several researchers have examined this issue by observing the responses of children to anger between others, which they term "background anger" (Cummings, 1987; Cummings, Iannotti, & Zahn-Waxler, 1985; Cummings, Zahn-Waxler, & Radke-Yarrow, 1981). The critical issue forming the basis for their work is whether the simple presence of discord affects children, even if they are not direct recipients or participants. Beginning in infancy and early toddlerhood, children seem both to be aware of others' negative emotions and to show an emotional reaction to such emotions. In the first of their series of investigations, Cummings et al. (1981) had mothers of infants and toddlers record both naturally occurring and simulated expressions of anger and affection by others in the family (i.e., the children were bystanders) and their children's reactions to those expressions. The researchers reported that expressions of anger by others in the family seemed to act as socioenvironmental stressors, which frequently caused distress in young children. (Such distress was even more apparent when verbal expressions were accompanied by physical attack of another family member.) They also found that repeated exposure to interparental anger increased the likelihood of these stress reactions in the offspring, and such children made more efforts to become actively involved in the conflict. Based on these initial data, the investigators hypothesized that exposure to harsh emotions threatens children's sense of security in relation to their social environment.

These researchers' second study (Cummings et al., 1985) involved slightly older (2-year-old) children, in which each target child and a familiar peer were exposed to background emotions of warmth and anger (displayed by unfamiliar actors in a family-styled laboratory setting). They found that children readily distinguished the two emotional expressions, and furthermore they responded to the angry adult interactions with significantly greater displays of distress and subsequent increases in aggression with their peers. (Distress was recorded on the basis of the child's body posture or movement, facial expression, voice, or cry; examples included the child attempting to mediate, showing concern, scolding, and fretting.) When the children were exposed for a second time to the actors' emotional exchanges one month later, the researchers found even higher levels of distress and aggressive behavior. Interestingly, boys showed more aggressive behavior than girls *following* the simulation, whereas girls showed more distress than boys *during* the simulation.

Similar distress reactions were noted when the study was repeated with slightly older (4- and 5-year-old) children (Cummings, 1987). In addition, however, the researchers were able to identify three types of responders on the basis of their behavioral reactions to adult arguments. "Concerned" emotional responders (46% of their sample) showed negative emotions concurrent with exposure, and later reported feeling sad and wanting to intervene. "Unresponsive" children (17%) showed no evidence of emotion, but later reported that they were angry. "Ambivalent" responders (35%) showed high emotional arousal during exposure (both positive and negative emotions). Later on, this latter group of children reported feeling happy, but they were most likely to become physically and verbally aggressive with their peers. Thus it appears that children's reactions to adult arguments and anger vary considerably, from strong displays of emotional distress to very hidden emotional reactions. Moreover, the type of immediate reaction shown by each child was associated with his or her own degree of anger, sadness, or aggression following the exposure.

The researchers raise two theoretical possibilities to explain these findings. The first explanation, termed "contagion of emotion," simply accounts for the child's emotional distress on the basis of being exposed to a stressful situation, that is, the actor's distress is acknowledged and reflected by the child. Their second explanation for these findings is based on the premise of the "transfer of excitation," in which emotional arousal occurs as a function of witnessing strong emotions, and such arousal leads to undercontrolled (e.g., aggressive) behavior. They point out that in this particular study children did not witness aggressive behavior, and, therefore, the results cannot be explained on the basis of modeling alone. Rather, the children witnessed a distressing verbal event that led to increased aggression on their part.

One question that emerges from these experimental findings regarding children's reactions to adult anger is this: How much conflict and anger can be experienced safely and without harm, given that each individual may differ in his or her reactions? Children must learn how to adapt to new situations, and such adaptation requires the development of coping abilities that are formed through continual exposure to mildly stressful, novel circumstances (Fagan, 1983). Despite this necessary adaptational process, it is clear that at some point exposure to strong emotions becomes a detrimental experience.

What Is Responsible for Violence? A Child's View of the Causes of Anger in Adults

The study of children's reactions to emotionally laden conflict situations also includes their cognitive interpretations of such events. Children may react unemotionally, for example, because they interpret the event to be insignificant or commonplace. Alternatively, some children may react to adult conflict with extreme emotional distress in part, as a result, of their belief that their mother and/or themselves are in grave jeopardy. The manner in which a child places "blame" for causing a harsh disagreement, physical fight, or similar emotion-charged interaction is influenced greatly by his or her developmental level and prior learning opportunities. As shown below through experimental analogue studies, younger children are less capable of looking for situational explanations or cues to assist them in interpreting the severity of a particular emotionally charged event. Accordingly, they are most likely to show the pattern of immediate distress that was noted in the NIMH series of studies. On the other hand, older children have learned to interpret events on the basis of situational as well as emotional cues. Such interpretations, therefore, are often influenced by the presence of verbal statements of blame (e.g., one adult blaming the other for the conflict), prior interpretations of similar events, and observable circumstances (e.g., an injury). Such interpretations are believed to have much significance in determining the manner in which a child will cope with similar stressful events in the near future (Van der Kolk, 1987).

One recent study investigated the manner in which children in three different age groups (5- to 6-year-olds, 7- to 9-year-olds, and 10- to 15-year-olds) attributed the sources of maternal anger and other emotions. Covell and Abramovitch (1987) asked these children to causally attribute their own and their mothers' happiness, sadness, and anger, and to indicate if and how they could change the way their mothers felt. They discovered that the younger group attributed maternal anger mostly to themselves only, in effect assuming responsibility for their mothers' emotions. Older children, on the other hand, attributed maternal anger to siblings, fathers, or events within the family in addition to themselves. The significance of children assuming responsibility for maternal anger and their believing themselves able to change maternal emotion is compounded when added to the NIMH findings reported above. That is, children show a noticeable stress reaction to emotional situations involving adults, and from an early age they tend to blame themselves for "causing" the displeasure. Such interpretations can be extremely resistant to change over time (Harter, 1982).

The explanation for the above findings is readily derived from existing knowledge of children's cognitive development. Children under age 8 tend to interpret most events in relation to the self. They may be unable to attend to more than one dimension of a situation (e.g., the angry expression), and, therefore, they have a distorted concept of what has transpired (Covell & Abramovitch, 1987). As well, they may have distorted concepts of causality as a result of their incomplete reasoning abilities; that is, events are not linked causally but more fortuitously. Covell and Abramovitch (in press) found that younger children (under age 8) had considerable difficulty explaining displaced maternal anger. Children could not explain why the story child was the recipient of maternal anger when its source was the story mother's spouse. This analogue is, of course, highly similar to the experiences of children in violent homes. Children (younger children especially) are likely to see only themselves as the sources of anger. Covell and Abramovitch (in press) suggest that children learn about causes of anger most readily when they are the culprit; however, mothers seldom explain why they are angry when the source is someone *other than the child* (see Crockenberg, 1985; Miller & Sperry, 1987). To explain their angry feelings to an inquisitive child, mothers may place blame on a distant source to avoid telling the child their true feelings (e.g., "I'm grumpy because of a bad day at work," rather than the truth, "I'm grumpy because I'm angry with dad."). In its naturally occurring context, when anger is unexpected and quite shocking to a child, he or she may not have the cognitive competence to take into account the whole situation. Placing blame for adult anger on oneself, therefore, is a developmentally defined common occurrence. The existence of such self-attributions among children of battered women has been noted, as reviewed below.

EMOTIONAL AND COGNITIVE DISORDERS AMONG CHILD WITNESSES

In addition to the externalizing of behavior problems, researchers have consistently found significantly higher levels of internalizing and over-controlled problem behaviors among shelter children (Hughes, Parkinson, & Vargo, 1987). Hughes (1986) reported that 55% of her sample of children residing in shelters were characterized as very withdrawn and 10% were described as having made suicidal gestures. The children showed signs of restlessness and nervousness, confusion because of the differences between home and school environments, reticence in discussing violence, and fantasies about a different home life. Similarly, Alessi and Hearn (1984) reported that a sample of children in a shelter for battered women often exhibited a high degree of anxiety, such as biting fingernails, pulling their hair, and somatic complaints of headaches and "tight" stomachs.

Again, sex differences have been examined with respect to internalizing behavior problems exhibited by children exposed to wife abuse. With some exceptions, girls are typically described as displaying more internalizing difficulties than boys. For example, Carlson (1984) describes girls as having an increasing assortment of somatic symptoms and being more likely than boys to become withdrawn, passive, cringing, and anxious.

Data from a four-month postshelter intake assessment indicated that the children had significantly more internalizing problems at shelter admission than they did four months later. These findings raise the possibility that assessments made shortly after the move to a shelter may not reflect later adjustment and recovery (Emery, Kraft, Joyce, & Shaw, 1984), but they nevertheless indicate the elevated signs of "crisis reaction" in these children.

In a further investigation, Hughes et al. (1987) found a relationship between the children's anxiety levels and the mothers' own anxiety levels, with the authors suggesting that the shelter children may be more "tuned in to" the feelings of their mothers so that, as their mothers' level of anxiety rises and falls, so does their own. Exposure to wife abuse has also been described as affecting children's social-cognitive development competence. For example, deLange (1986) observed that children in shelters were often socially isolated from their peers and did not relate to the activities or interests of their age group. She estimated that approximately 40% of these children had problems interacting with other children or with adults.

Yet in a recent study, Cassady, Allen, Lyon, and McGeehan (1987) concluded that no clear patterns of relationships between exposure to parental violence and children's social behavior have emerged, based on the limited number of studies. One study (Rosenberg, 1984) found normal levels of social competence in child witnesses, while another (Wolfe et al., 1985) found lower levels of social competence. No differences in social competence between child witnesses and a community sample have been found in several other studies (e.g., Hughes & Hampton, 1984; Kraft, Sullivan-Hanson, Christopoulos, Cohn, & Emery, 1984; Woods, 1981).

In a related area, the social problem-solving abilities of children exposed to wife abuse have started to receive some attention. An initial study by Rosenberg (1984) compared the social problem-solving abilities of a group of children, 5 to 8 years of age, who are witnessed wife abuse, with a group of children from nonviolent families. Results suggested that children who were witnesses to wife abuse tended to choose either passive or aggressive strategies to resolve interpersonal conflict and were less likely to choose assertive strategies. In addition, children exposed to higher frequencies and intensities of wife abuse performed significantly less well on a measure of interpersonal sensitivity—the ability to understand social situations and the thoughts and feelings of persons involved in those situations—than did those children exposed to less frequent and intense wife abuse.

In an elaboration of Rosenberg's study, Grossier (1986) studied the impact of exposure to videotapes of mild and strong anger on the social-cognitive skills of children from violent and nonviolent families. The children from violent families were found to have more difficulties in resolving interpersonal problems when they encountered obstacles to their initial solutions compared with children from nonviolent families. In addition, results suggested that children's observations of parental conflict-resolution strategies related to their own choice of problem-resolution strategies when viewing videotapes of peer conflict. Children exposed to high levels of wife abuse gave fewer constructive (e.g., direct discussion, assertive action, mutual compromise) and more nonconstructive (e.g., verbal and physical aggression, passive resolution) strategies to resolve peer conflict. This finding again implies that children's perceptions of social situations may be distorted as a function of their negative family experiences.

Children exposed to wife abuse have also been described as being at risk for a number of school adjustment difficulties. For example, in a sample of children living in a shelter for battered women, Hughes (1986) found that children often had difficulties with school, including poor academic performance, school phobia, and difficulties in concentration that affected the schoolwork of young school-age children. Similarly, McKay (1981) described such children as constantly fighting with peers, rebelling against adult instruction and authority, and being unwilling to do school work.

SUBTLE SYMPTOMS: CHILDREN'S ATTITUDES AND EMOTIONAL EXPRESSION

Because children who witness their mother being assaulted by their father are experiencing a traumatic life event, some of these children will reflect this experience through obvious adjustment problems that demonstrate a significant disruption in their emotional and cognitive development. Some of these social difficulties will overlap with those observed in children who have experienced traumatic events related to serious disruptions and chaos in their families. However, children living with violence in their family may exhibit some specific problem areas that relate uniquely to this experience. Sometimes these problem areas are not immediately apparent unless specific information is requested from children or they are observed in specific situations. These problem areas can be called the "subtle symptoms" of witnessing wife assault, because they often require careful investigation to detect. Additionally, these subtle symptoms may be present in children who do not demonstrate any of the more dramatic emotional and behavioral adjustment problems.

These subtle symptoms can be classified into three major areas, related to (a) responses and attitudes about conflict resolution, (b) assigning responsibility for violence, and (c) knowledge and skills in dealing with violent incidents. To better understand these symptoms, consider the following case illustrations:

> Mary and Nicole, age 8 and 9 years of age, were described by shelter staff as ideal young girls in terms of their behavior and social competence. Although they had witnessed violence in two families since they were born, both girls were high achievers in school and reported by their teachers to be popular with peers and involved in many extracurricular activities. They often spoke of returning to their home while in the shelter and indicated that they missed their father and the many favorite belongings left behind. When asked about why they came to leave home they both stated that if their mother kept the house tidier and had supper ready to time, their father wouldn't have to hit her so often.

> John presented himself as a mature adolescent who was very supportive of his mother and younger siblings while they adjusted to the shelter. He appeared to be a positive role model for the younger children in the house by his ability to comply with the rules and help newer residents in crisis cope with crowded surroundings. He rarely spoke of his father. When encouraged to discuss his feelings about the violence he witnessed, he expressed his disgust and anger. When asked about his plans to deal with these feelings he disclosed an elaborate plot "to get even" with his father by poisoning him.

Louise was only a few years old but she was very advanced in her social judgment and verbal skills. She demonstrated a wide range of affect, which she utilized to distract her mother and other shelter residents from the pain and sadness that they displayed. She said she knew why she had come to the shelter. Louise claimed that she kept leaving her tricycle on the front walk, contrary to her father's repeated instruction. "One day I got him so mad that he hit mom." Louise was sure she was to blame for the violence.

Tom faced a terrible dilemma. He was only 7 years old, and he had to judge whether or not his father was going to shoot his mother. His father often picked up the shotgun and threatened his mother whenever he was jealous and thought she might leave. His mother could usually talk him into putting away the gun or call his grandmother to come and talk sense into father. Tonight seemed different. His father seemed more upset than usual and yelled at his mother that he would kill her so nobody else could ever marry her. Tom decided to go to the neighbors to get them to call the police. The police came and used skilled negotiations to avert a tragedy. Tom's father went to jail for six months for threatening his mother and for dangerous use of a weapon. Tom told the shelter staff that he ruined his father's life by calling the police. "If it wasn't for me, he wouldn't have a criminal record, and maybe my mother would have stayed with him."

Straus and his colleagues (Straus et al., 1980) pointed out that children in violent homes learn several important lessons about conflict resolution. They are taught that violence is an appropriate way of resolving conflict in intimate relationships. These children learn that assaultive behavior and threats are very effective means to maintain power and control over other people. They will acquire all the rationalizations about this violence being an essential strategy whenever there is too much stress or too many problems to address. In any event, children learn that the victims of the violence have brought this consequence upon themselves by their own behavior or by the fact that they are devalued by being a woman.

Many children will demonstrate the lessons they have learned by the way they fight with peers in the playground or by the hostility with which they greet discipline from female teachers. The more subtle symptoms, however, relate to attitudes about violence and the children's inability to hold men responsible for their behavior and to understand how women can become trapped by financial, social, and psychological restraints. Mary and Nicole in the first illustration have accepted that their mother is to blame for the violence. One can speculate about how this view may be the early seeds for their own future victimization in marriage.

John in the second illustration appears trapped by the very behavior that disgusts him. He cannot stand his father's behavior, but he is actively pursuing a strategy of silent violence to solve his problem. His thoughts may be grounded in the reality that no one in the community has been able to terminate the violence in his family, and his sense of hopelessness may drive him to a desperate plan of action.

Children of battered women may also accept an exaggerated sense of responsibility for the violence in their family. This subtle symptom relates to the absurd notion that they have caused the violence by their own behavior and are, therefore, the author of their parents' fate. They may also feel that it is their responsibility to prevent the violence by defusing their father's anger and protecting their mother. Louise, in the third case illustration, is unfortunately typical of many young children we have interviewed. They feel that they have to be perfect. Like Louise, one tricycle in the wrong place at the wrong time can be the trigger for a violent episode. From our interviews with children, these thoughts seem deeply ingrained and persistent over many years.

The fourth case illustration reflects the complex issues around the safety of children and their mothers. Tom requires basic knowledge and skills to handle an emergency that hasn't been covered in school courses on fire, accident, and traffic safety. He has to assess the lethality of a situation and judge the possibility of his mother's life being in serious danger. When will the fight start? Where will it end? Who will look after my younger brothers and sisters? How long will it take for the police to come? What number do I dial? Will my father be even angrier at me or my mother? The list of questions can be very lengthy, and the time frame for action may be one of seconds.

Children like Tom face a double challenge in not only having to have specific knowledge and skills to handle a crisis but also deciding whether or not to use this response. Although our initial speculation about children of battered women was that their life responses would require them to learn about who to call and what to do, field experience revealed the very opposite. Many children lacked basic information about community resources for emergencies and had poor experiences in previous attempts to get help (e.g., slow and disinterested police response). Some children knew what to do but felt paralyzed by a loyalty conflict between protecting their mother or betraying their father.

The subtle symptoms discussed above have several implications for the assessment of and intervention planning for children of battered women. Eliciting and understanding their symptoms requires specific areas to be explored in interviews. A structured child interview to address these questions is outlined in Chapter 4 as well as intervention strategies to begin to help a child recover from exposure to this violence.

SUMMARY

Chapter 2 has provided some understanding of the wide range of behavioral, emotional, and cognitive adjustment problems encountered in child witnesses to wife abuse. The chapter has stressed that it is important to consider normal child development and the manner in which all children look to parents as models. Parents fulfill a role as pillars for the foundation of their children's learning. When their experience at home centers on violence and its physical and emotional aftermath, children's development can be affected dramatically. In Chapter 3, the mechanisms by which living with violence affects children's adjustment will be explored.

3

UNDERSTANDING THE IMPACT OF TRAUMATIC EVENTS IN THE LIVES OF CHILDREN

Based on the clinical and empirical findings to date, children who are exposed to wife abuse are decidedly at an increased risk of developing adjustment problems. This vulnerability may be the result of several inter-related factors, including their exposure to violent role models, experiencing the discord that accompanies wife abuse, the lack of physically and emotionally available caregivers, and/or the fear that their mothers or they may be physically injured (Rosenbaum & O'Leary, 1981). The difficulties that children often face as an accompaniment to family violence may be further exacerbated for those children who are brought to shelters for victims of domestic violence. Children in shelters are likely to have experienced a complete disruption in their social support systems, particularly with their school, friends, neighborhood, and usually the significant adult male in their lives.

The specific manner in which exposure to wife assault is harmful to children, however, cannot be fully determined on the basis of the research findings to date. While studies have indicated that children who are exposed to stressful events are at a higher risk for psychopathology, results have not suggested that there is a specific pattern of child disturbance associated with a particular stressor. However, theoretical developments and evidence from related child populations can be drawn upon to advance the current understanding of children from violent families. For example, the specific *type* of stressor may not be as critical to the child's adaptation as the *amount* of stressors and the child's perception of them. Rutter (1979) discovered that, when children had only one risk factor in their lives (for example, a psychiatrically disturbed parent), the child was no more likely to have a psychiatric disorder than children who had no risk factors present at all. However, children who had two risk factors occurring simultaneously (for example, family poverty and an alcoholic parent) were four times more at risk for developing a psychiatric disturbance. Rutter described this interaction between the number of stressors and negative developmental impact as a "potentiating" effect, in which the combination of different stressors produced damaging effects that were more significant than one would assume on the basis of the individual stressors alone. Similar findings were reported by Rae-Grant, Boyle, Offord, and Thomas (1984), who also showed that the more risk factors there were in the child's life (e.g., parent-child separation, domestic violence, parental deviance), the greater was the child's risk of adjustment problems. These researchers differed from Rutter (1979) somewhat in their interpretation, arguing instead that the summative effects of stressors are more damaging to child development than the potentiating effect of the combination of chronic stressors.

Although recognizable patterns of child adjustment have not been found to correlate with exposure to particular stressors, it is feasible to assume that each stressful event or circumstance has some unique impact on children. To explore this issue of how different stressors in childhood affect development, and relate these comparative findings to children of battered women, this chapter looks first at two theoretical notions underlying much of the research on the topic of developmental psychopathology: the cycle-of-violence hypothesis and the family disruption hypothesis. A summary of the evidence supporting and opposing each of these views is presented for the purpose of formulating a theoretical and conceptual framework for understanding the impact of family violence on children's adjustment. Presented next is a discussion of the related literature on children's coping reactions to other traumatic events, which offers additional clarity in terms of how children react and cope with family problems that are similar in nature to family violence but that differ in important dimensions.

EXPLAINING THE RELATIONSHIP BETWEEN FAMILY VIOLENCE AND CHILDREN'S ADJUSTMENT

The Cycle-of-Violence Hypothesis

One of the most familiar and widely accepted views of aggressive behavior in children and adults is the belief that "violence breeds violence." The cycle-of-violence hypothesis, derived in large part from social learning theory, suggests that a child who learns violent behavior patterns at home will be more likely to engage in similar patterns later on. This linear relationship (i.e., victims of violence become perpetrators of violence) is relatively straightforward and is attractive in large part because of its ability to account for the higher rates of aggressive and violent behavior often described among children from violent families. Despite some criticisms, this hypothesis contains several issues that are paramount to the target population and that deserve consideration of the supportive evidence.

The cycle-of-violence (or, alternatively, the intergenerational transmission of violence) assumption originated in part from the rationale that physical aggression in the home provides both a model for learning aggressive behavior and a supportive environment that views such behavior as appropriate. By being participant members of a violent family, each new generation of children learns how to be violent toward their own family members (Straus et al., 1980). Before presenting the findings based on clinical populations, a brief overview is given of the laboratory-based studies that were designed to test a central assumption of this model—that exposure to aggressive models results in increased levels of aggressive behavior in the observers at a considerable point later on in their development.

The Influence of Exposure to Aggressive Models

The issue of how children learn to aggress toward others has been widely studied from the perspective of vicarious observational learning, or modeling (Bandura, 1973). At the forefront of much of this effort have been investigations looking at the effects of violent, aggressive models viewed by children through constant observation of television shows. It is reasoned that, if it can be demonstrated that at least some children learn to become more aggressive and violent as a function of the type and amount of television viewed, this finding would have considerable implications for those children who witness violence by important members of their own family firsthand.

In a recent review of television violence and its relation to the cycle-of-violence hypothesis, Widom (1989) points out that exposure to television violence has been determined to lead to increased levels of aggression in some viewers, to have long-term effects as well as effects immediately after exposure, and to lead to emotional desensitization. Such desensitization, it is believed, makes the viewer less likely to respond both psychologically and behaviorally to aggression in others (i.e., less and less emotional reaction to violence on television is detected, and the observer appears to have habituated to the initial arousal). Widom notes as well that heavy television viewing may lead to distorted perceptions about real-life violence among both adults and children.

Using field methodology, Heath, Kruttschnitt, and Ward (1986) examined the relationship between self-reported television viewing (i.e., number and type of shows watched) at ages 8, 10, and 12 years and the consequent commission of violent criminal acts. Based on a sample of 48 male inmates who were incarcerated for violent acts and 45 nonviolent, nonincarcerated males (matched on age, race, and residence), these researchers found that the extent of a person's reported television viewing was not, by itself, predictive of violent acts. Rather, it was the interaction of large amounts of television viewing and exposure to maternal or parental abuse that related highly to violent crime. Apparently, the combination of real and simulated violence was a significantly more potent influence in the development of violent crime than either alone. These findings, and others similar in design and conclusions, led Friedrich-Cofer and Huston (1986, p. 368) to conclude from their review of this topic that "the weight of the evidence from different methods of investigation supports the hypothesis that television violence affects aggression. Virtually all reviewers agree that laboratory studies of children and adults demonstrate positive findings and that field surveys produce modest but consistently positive correlations."

In commenting on this relationship between the passive observation of violence on television and the active participation in violent acts later on in life, Lowrey and DeFleur (1988) make an important distinction between the child's acquisition and his or her acceptance of aggressive behavior. That is, a child may observe and remember novel behavior without necessarily performing that behavior. Although observational learning does not necessarily lead to action, it makes more likely the performance of otherwise unlikely responses. The potential range of behavior that a child (or, later, an adolescent or adult) may display when provoked or under stress (especially in a new situation) is increased through exposure to more extreme, violent models. Similar to the conclusions drawn in reference to children's television viewing, Lowrey and DeFleur (1988) stress that there is no doubt that children are exposed to violence and no doubt that they can learn by viewing television. What is missing, however, is an adequate explanation describing the conditions under which an observer will accept such behavior as a guide to his or her own actions. One major hypothesis concerning this missing connection is that the continued witnessing of violent episodes (especially across different contexts) increases the willingness of children to be aggressors as well as increasing the magnitude of the aggressive response. Unfortunately, at the present time there is not sufficient information available to be able to determine accurately what child characteristics and conditions (e.g., age, sex, heredity, environmental context) are likely to be most vulnerable to the negative influence of exposure to violent models.

Supportive Evidence and Conclusions for the Cycle-of-Violence Hypothesis

In addressing this hypothesis, researchers have frequently studied the abusive backgrounds of adults and children and related such events to their subsequent violence as adolescents and as parents. Because most of these studies are retrospective, lack control, and often fail to look carefully at the "survivors," the conclusions supporting the cycle-of-violence notions are limited (Widom, 1989). Yet, overall, there seems to be a higher likelihood of abuse by parents if they themselves were abused as children (compared with those who were not abused in childhood). Estimates of abused children who become abusive parents range from a low of 7% to a high of 70%, with an estimated rate of intergenerational transmission to be 30%, ± 5% (Kaufman & Zigler, 1987; Widom, 1989).

An even stronger association between childhood victims of violence and subsequent "victimizers" emerges in studies looking at the relationship between child maltreatment (abuse and neglect, in particular) and the commission of violent crimes. In Widom's (1989) review of 12 studies of delinquent populations, she found that the more-violent adolescent males were more likely to have experienced abuse, or to have witnessed extreme physical abuse, compared with nonviolent males. An example of the strength of this relationship is shown in a large-scale study, conducted by Geller and Ford-Somma in 1984, of 226 incarcerated juvenile offenders (cited in Widom, 1989). It is not surprising that these researchers found that the extent of family violence (where children were either passive or active victims) was quite high among their sample of 182 boys and 42 girls. Their regression analyses revealed, however, that *routine violence* was the strongest predictor of violent delinquent behavior. Routine violence in childhood, defined as the estimated number of times the child was hit by an object, was even more predictive of later violence than was either life-threatening violence (i.e., the number of times the child was threatened or assaulted with a weapon) or injurious violence (i.e., the number of times the child was beaten resulting in physical injuries).

Based on their work with similar delinquent populations, Fagan and Wexler (1987) estimate that between 20% and 40% of families of chronically violent adolescents had experienced marital violence (depending on the reporting source), approximately 25% had hit the child with an object, and almost 40% of parents had been arrested. Although the base rate for violence in this particular population must be taken into account when considering these figures, the preponderance of evidence supports the conclusion that the family histories of violent offenders are characterized by high rates of neglect, physical and psychological abuse, and parental deviancy (Henggeler, 1989).

Finally, support for the cycle-of-violence hypothesis is derived from studies of children of battered women. Extending the laboratory findings on the impact on children of viewing aggressive behavior, field studies like those cited in the previous chapter have noted the association between exposure to parental violence in childhood and subsequent violent behavior in the community and at home. For example, Lewis, Shanok, Pincus, and Glaser (1979) noted that 79% of violent children in institutions reported that they had witnessed extreme violence between their parents, whereas only 20% of the nonviolent offenders did so. In one of the few studies that explored the relationship between type of violence (i.e., passively observed or directly received), Kalmuss (1984) used survey data from adults and found that observing aggression and violence between parents was more strongly related to involvement in severe marital violence than was being a victim of abuse during adolescence. Furthermore, the problem of marital violence in adulthood increased dramatically when, as adolescents, respondents had experienced both types of family violence.

Despite these convincing associations between childhood violence and the expression of violence in adulthood, however, there are a number of methodological considerations that make firm conclusions regarding the adequacy of this model somewhat difficult. Such considerations as the reliance on retrospective accounts of violence, reliance on parental report, correlational (noncausal) designs, the lack of appropriate comparison groups, and similar drawbacks to testing the hypothesis warrant caution in drawing any conclusions (Widom, 1989). However, a reasonable conclusion acknowledges that there is, indeed, an impact on children's development from being a passive or active victim of (chronic) violence in childhood, a relationship that is significant but is not all encompassing. Other mechanisms need to be discovered that help to explain why violence in childhood affects some children more than others and why it affects them in different ways.

The Family Disruption Hypothesis

Whereas the cycle-of-violence hypothesis has received indirect support from a number of sources, it remains incomplete as a theory of interpersonal violence because of its lack of confirmed mechanisms that account for how such intergenerational transmission takes place. It relies heavily on the direct influence of violent models on children's behavior, an issue that undoubtedly is viable but that fails to explain some of the other possible mechanisms that may *indirectly* affect children's development in violent families. That is, exposure to family violence may not only have a *direct* influence on the child's ongoing development (e.g., by teaching the child how to use aggressive problem-solving tactics) but its existence in the family is likely to set into motion a number of related, significant events that singly or in combination operate to disrupt the child's normal developmental progress. Accordingly, the negative impact of wife abuse on children's development can come from both direct and indirect sources within and outside of the family.

The concept of how family dysfunction affects children both directly and indirectly is not new; rather, it has been a cornerstone of family systems theory for many years. However, few researchers in the field of family violence have attempted to address these indirect mechanisms and pathways within the family; most have chosen instead to demonstrate the more direct, cycle-of-violence, connections. In a recent paper, Emery (1989) describes the family systems model in reference to children's reactions to family conflict. The first presumed step in the model is that family conflict serves as an aversive event that creates distress in the child. In response, the child reacts emotionally (e.g., becomes fearful, sad) and/or instrumentally (e.g., runs away from home, intervenes in the conflict) in an attempt to alleviate the distress. It is this second aspect of the theory that has been the major focus of much of the research to date, following the belief that the child's actions are maladaptive. The child's actions may be functional, however, to the extent that they reduce the conflict or draw the attention of the parents toward the child's demands. Consequently, such actions are likely to be maintained because of the function they serve for the child and for the entire family. It should be emphasized, however, that despite their intermittent success at reducing conflict, some of these actions may indeed be maladaptive for the child, such as his or her increased aggressiveness, poor schoolwork, and so on.

The disruption hypothesis is one that is derived from both social-learning and from family systems theories, in that it predicts that major (negative) events in the family serve to disrupt the child's normal routine (e.g., sources of reward and punishment, structure, activities), thus creating a need for the child to adapt quickly to new circumstances. Moreover, the actual source of such disruption may be several steps removed from the child's immediate concern – he or she must face changes/stressors that are the *by-products* of major family events, in addition to the direct disruption usually created by the events themselves. In this manner, stressful family events, such as wife abuse, create an atmosphere in which the child not only faces the immediate threat of danger, fear, and unpredictable adults, he or she must also learn to cope with the myriad forms of "fallout" from the conflict, such as parental ineffectiveness, changes in residence and family income, sibling distress, and many others. The disruption hypothesis, therefore, accounts for the adjustment problems of children of battered women on the basis of their attempts to cope with extremely unpredictable and far-reaching changes in the family unit.

The mechanisms by which children's development is affected are contained in the two developmental processes described in Chapter 2: the child's ongoing training in both behavioral and emotional expression by significant members of the family. In both processes, it is believed that the primary caregiver (usually the mother) serves as the mediator of the child's adjustment; that is, the mother delivers the consequences that shape the child's behavior, and she emits the emotional expressions that cue the child as to the significance of a particular event or expression. As Patterson et al. (1989, p. 332) postulate, "the major impact of stress on child adjustment is mediated by family management practices. If stressors disrupt parenting practices, then the child is placed at risk for adjustment problems." Nontrivial disruptions in family management practices are especially likely to occur when the parents already possess minimal skill at managing crises and/or engage in antisocial behavior and ineffective coping activities (e.g., abusive drinking). According to Patterson, it is these disruptions that are thought to place the child at risk for adjustment problems.

In short, this model accounts for the negative effect of family violence on the child in two ways: (a) directly, through training of the child by exposing him or her to deviant behavioral and emotional expression, and (b) indirectly, by the absence of consistent, effective child management and family functioning (caused in large part by the decline in the mother's parenting capacity). Moreover, the child's behavior plays a reciprocal role in maintaining the family dysfunction, in terms of placing counterstress upon the marital relationship and upon the mother's child-rearing abilities.

These theoretical links between family violence and children's developmental disorders are diagramed in Figure 3.1. At the top of the figure is a box representing the occurrence of wife abuse. In a direct manner, such exposure to wife abuse can create stress on the child, resulting in his or her attempts at coping. These attempts on the part of the child are seen most often in terms of increased behavioral and emotional symptoms (shown by the solid arrow pointing from "wife abuse" to "child's stress and coping responses" in the figure). Other direct effects of witnessing wife assault can include an increase in the child's aggressive behavior as a result of modeling by father and issues regarding the child's own safety. In return, the child's behavioral and emotional reactions to the violence can create additional stress on the marital relationship, thus aggravating the volatile situation even further (shown by the dashed-line arrow). Wife abuse can also create a number of problems in the family that are likely to pose added stress on the child in an indirect fashion. Wife abuse creates stress on the mother, leading to her attempts to cope (shown by the solid arrow on the left-hand side of the figure). Similar to the child's reaction, the mother may exhibit increased physical and psychological symptoms indicative of uncontrollable, stressful events as a direct result of the abuse. Her child management effectiveness will almost certainly be reduced because of the family discord and emotional turmoil that result from wife assault. The direct, negative impact of wife abuse on the mother may then be met by a reciprocal force on the marital relationship as well as on the parent-child relationship, as shown in Figure 3.1. Furthermore, the mother's reduced ability places added strain on the parent-child relationship, further aggravating the child's futile attempts to cope with the overwhelming negative events in the family. Parental ineffectiveness, when coupled with urgent child needs for greater parental attention and stability, provides a further ingredient in the recipe for child disturbance, again resulting in large part from the fallout from wife abuse.

Supportive Evidence and Conclusions for the Family Disruption Hypothesis

As a part of a systemic theory of family process, this particular hypothesis primarily addresses the indirect linkages between wife abuse and children's adjustment. The *direct* influences on the child (e.g., increased behavioral and emotional symptoms, imitative modeling of aggression, and safety issues) need little further explanation, for this pathway has been demonstrated to account for a significant percentage of variance in children's adjustment (e.g., Wolfe et al., 1985). Evidence supporting the indirect, disruptive influence of family violence on children's adjustment is, however, a bit more difficult to gather because of the large number of factors that must be taken into consideration. Furthermore, as is true for most research dealing with private, relatively infrequent events in the family, one must rely heavily on the interpretation of correlational findings that cannot imply causality. Therefore, most of the initial findings addressing these indirect influences must be interpreted with caution until additional support is forthcoming.

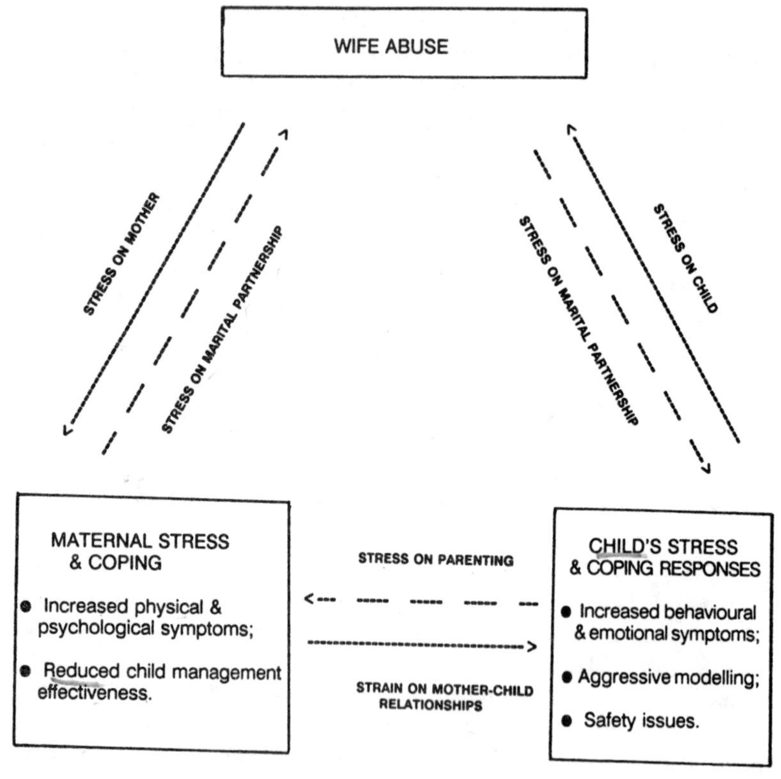

Figure 3.1. The Links Between Wife Abuse and Children's Developmental Disorders

These methodological issues notwithstanding, the two primary pathways that constitute the indirect influence of family violence on the child have received initial confirmation in recent empirical studies. The first pathway, depicting the increased stress on the mother (see Figure 3.1), has been confirmed in studies of battered women. Compared with matched control groups of nonbattered women, women residing in shelters are found to be extremely elevated on stress-related scales of physical and psychological symptomatology, such as somatic complaints, anxiety and insomnia, and depression (Jaffe, Wolfe, Wilson, & Zak, 1986). The Battered Woman's Syndrome, which shares a strong resemblance to prisoner of war symptoms, has been described as a prolonged pattern of depressed affect and a general sense of helplessness, fear, and social withdrawal (Walker, 1979). These elevated symptoms are significantly related to other stressors in their lives, most notably the degree of negative life events they have experienced during the past year (Jaffe, Wolfe, Wilson, & Zak, 1986). It is not surprising that such events are intricately related to violence in the family, such as moves, separation, police involvement, and problems at work.

Empirical support for the second pathway, depicting the mother's reduced effectiveness and the strain on the parent-child relationship, has been shown preliminarily in two multivariate studies involving large samples of battered women and their children. It is also noteworthy that these two independent studies drew participants from entirely different settings: women who had gone to shelters for protection/assistance (Wolfe et al., 1986) and couples who had requested marital therapy at a university clinic (Jouriles, Murphy, & O'Leary, 1989). In the study by Wolfe et al. (1986), women (approximately one-half from shelters and one-half from the community) completed information about their own adjustment and that of their children (ages 6-16). These also described the type and amount of violence that they and their children had been exposed to and provided information pertaining to the level of family stability (e.g., number of moves and marital separations over the past two years, the child's school changes, and income changes). When children's internalizing and externalizing behavior problems were predicted on the basis of the amount and severity of wife abuse alone (i.e., direct impact on the child), less than 10% of the variance in behavior could be explained. However, when measures of the level of maternal stress (e.g., self-reported health and emotional problems, plus negative life events and family crises) were added to the equation as mediators of children's adjustment (i.e., the indirect impact on the child associated with disruption), children's adjustment levels were explained more significantly (19% of the explained variance). This finding led the authors to surmise that the child's level of adjustment could be due not only to the direct influence of being exposed to wife abuse but that it might be assessed more accurately in terms of the extent of the mother's successful or unsuccessful coping responses. Battered women who reported extreme anxiety, sleeping problems, somatic complaints, and similar stress-related dysfunction were significantly more likely to have children who were exhibiting clinically elevated levels of adjustment problems.

Jouriles et al. (1989) addressed the family disruption hypothesis from a slightly different perspective, drawing upon the extensive literature on children's adjustment to marital discord, separation, and divorce. They were interested in determining whether child adjustment problems were a function of marital discord in general (i.e., problems in the relationship) or whether they were specific to marital aggression occurring in the relationship *above and beyond* discord. Therefore, their study did not actually test the notion of disruption or indirect pathways per se, but instead it defined more precisely the nature of the adult interactions that were most responsible for child adjustment disorders. The study involved 87 couples who had requested marital therapy and who had children between 5 and 12 years of age. The researchers discovered that marital aggression or violence, as measured by the Conflict Tactics Scale, contributed unique variance to the prediction of child conduct disorders, personality disorders, inadequate-maturity characteristics, and clinical levels of problematic child behavior, even after controlling for marital discord, child's age and sex, and the interaction of child's age and marital discord. Although these findings once again cannot, by themselves, be interpreted unequivocally as evidence favoring the disruption model, they demonstrate quite strongly the significant impact of wife abuse on the family unit.

Based on the preliminary findings of these studies involving children of battered women and their families, it is possible to cautiously endorse an explanatory model of children's adjustment that takes into account the two major premises of the cycle-of-violence and the family disruption hypotheses. These premises, generally speaking, correspond to the assumption that family violence affects children's adjustment in both direct and indirect ways. Because these phenomena are not open to experimental manipulation, nor can these children and their mothers be readily involved in research, it will take considerably more investigation to confirm and fine-tune these assumptions. Nevertheless, the evidence supporting the supposition that children are affected by wife abuse through a pyramid network of fallout suggests that this issue may pose considerably more concern for children's long-term adjustment than has been previously assumed. Moreover, this model offers an important additional source of prevention and intervention ideas beyond those suggested on the basis of direct effects alone. For example, in addition to being negatively affected by his or her mother's poor level of functioning, a child's recovery and adjustment from family violence may also be positively mediated by his or her mother's successful coping resources. Efforts extended to assist battered women and to prevent family violence, therefore, would be well spent in helping the child recover from or avoid the impact as well, as is discussed further in Chapter 4.

RELATED LITERATURE ON CHILDREN'S COPING REACTIONS TO TRAUMATIC EVENTS

Efforts to explain and intervene in the adjustment problems of children of battered woman can benefit from the extensive literature on related trauma and coping in childhood. In many ways, children of battered women are not entirely unique in their suffering but share many aspects of family life in common with children who have an alcoholic parent or an abusive parent, or who witness homicide or other extremely disturbing events. The following section discusses several prominent areas in the literature that have looked at children's coping reactions to traumatic events. Similarities to the present focus of attention are pointed out as they appear.

Other Traumatic Events in Childhood

Marital Discord, Separation, and Divorce.

The study of the impact of marital conflict and parental separation and divorce is most salient to the population of children exposed to wife abuse, because children in violent homes may experience these events and vice versa. There is mounting evidence that children's adjustment can be negatively affected by parental separation and divorce. For example, Kelly and Wallerstein (1976) and Wallerstein and Kelly (1980) studied the impact of divorce on 57 latency-age children shortly after their parents separated and again one year after the separation. At the initial interview, the children were described as presenting a variety of difficulties adjusting to the family separation, including a rise in aggression and irritability, intense anger directed toward one or both parents, fears of abandonment, and loneliness. At the one-year follow-up, approximately half of the children continued to present the same amount of or more serious difficulties in their adjustment. Similarly, Hetherington, Cox, and Cox (1979) compared children from recently divorced families with children from intact families. They found that the children from the divorced families were more dependent, disobedient, aggressive, whiny, demanding, and unaffectionate than were children from the intact families.

Strong associations have also been found in clinical populations between marital discord (not necessarily violence) and child behavior problems (Christensen, Phillips, Glasgow, & Johnson, 1983; Porter & O'Leary, 1980). For example, Porter and O'Leary found a significant correlation ($r = 0.40$) between overt marital hostility and boys' conduct disorders. Similarly, Christensen et al. (1983) found that marital discord accounted for 25% of the variance in child behavior problems (e.g., alienation, social nonconformity, depression) in their clinical sample.

Similar associations between marital discord and child adjustment difficulties have been reported with nonclinical populations. For example, Slater and Haber (1984) found that ongoing high conflict in intact or divorced homes produced lowered self-esteem, greater anxiety, and less of a feeling of control among the children. In a review article on children from divorced and discordant homes, Emery (1982) concluded that children in homes in which there is interparental conflict are at greater risk than children from intact or broken homes that are relatively conflict-free. He also suggested that both the amount and type of interparental conflict to which the child is exposed are important determinants of the effect of conflict on the children.

Physical, Emotional, and Sexual Abuse of Children

These overlapping forms of child maltreatment each represent trauma to the developing child, mostly in terms of their psychological, as opposed to physical, impact. Each type of maltreatment has been associated with a greater likelihood of particular developmental disturbances, such as increased aggression among physically abused children (Wolfe, 1987), disturbances in sexual development and self-esteem among sexually abused children (Wolfe & Wolfe, 1988), and poor peer relationships among emotionally abused children (Hart & Brassard, 1987). However, it is widely acknowledged that these different forms of maltreatment also give rise to many of the same developmental adjustment problems, suggesting that very similar psychological processes may be commonly responsible for the children's reactions to trauma. That is, the emotional trauma resulting from chronic rejection, loss of affection, betrayal, and feelings of helplessness that accompanies child maltreatment may be a common factor accounting for the changes in child behavior.

Wolfe (1987) suggested that a process involving conditioned emotional responses and attributions for traumatic events may be operative with children who are mistreated by their caregivers. Emotionally based reactions at the time of the event, such as fear, panic, and apprehension, are associated (in time or context) with particular persons, places, or events, creating conditioned emotional responses that may recur incessantly in the presence of eliciting stimuli (such as a picture of the person, reminders of the circumstances, or proximity to the place where the event occurred). In addition, children's emotional reactions will lead to attempts to "search for meaning" for the events, especially because the unpleasant feelings are associated with significant members of the child's own family. In so doing, it is believed that some children will shift the blame to persons or circumstances that they find more acceptable than members of their own family. Over time, therefore, maltreated children may develop wrong attributions for their experiences that place blame on innocent parties (especially themselves) and that serve to justify maladaptive, self-defeating behaviors toward themselves (e.g., low self-esteem) or toward others (e.g., antisocial acts). This explanation of the processes underlying children's reactions to maltreatment may help to account for the wide-ranging and unpredictable adjustment reactions seen among child victims of various types of maltreatment.

The knowledge gained by the study of children's emotional and behavioral reactions to physical and sexual abuse is applicable to children who are indirect victims of abuse as well. It is reasoned that emotional reactions are elicited in children who directly or indirectly witness wife abuse, requiring them to develop explanations and coping reactions to these traumata. This argument rests in part on the presumed importance of the family as the child's major socialization context, thereby creating unpleasant and disquieting feelings in the child as a consequence of violence between parents or significant adults in the family. Despite some important differences between physical abuse, sexual abuse, emotional abuse, and exposure to wife abuse, the family dynamics, structures, and intergenerational features are common to all four types (see Van der Kolk, 1987).

Children of War

War represents an event of extraordinary intensity that is sudden, dramatic, difficult to control, and unanticipated, that produces personal uprooting, loss and separation, family disruption, mental and physical suffering, and enormous social change (Garmezy, 1983). Thus studies of children of war afford some comparison with children of violent families.

In a recent review article of children's adjustment following war, Ayalon and Van Tassel (1987) reported that children observed during and after World War II often showed *fewer* psychologically traumatic symptoms than adults did. Of the children exposed to severe stressors, many were able to adapt fairly well in a relatively short time, although residual effects such as increased sensitivity and vulnerability to minor environmental change remained. The factors that seemed to influence children's ability to cope with the stressors associated with war included their age, temperament, and relationship with family before and during the war (Ayalon & Van Tassel, 1987). Apparently, despite the severity and intensity of war, children often cope adaptively. Such positive coping, it is reasoned, is largely a function of family cohesion and uniform support of the external conflict, which facilitate children's sense of security and assistance.

However, reports summarized by Langmeier and Matejcek in 1975 (cited in Garmezy, 1983) indicated that while children may have quickly recovered from any physical health disruption associated with war, their social behavior remained more of a long-term concern. They cited how the behavior of children in concentration camps quickly deteriorated. They stole, cheated, formed gangs, and engaged in various forms of antisocial behavior. Mental disorders, in contrast to antisocial behavior, were an infrequent occurrence; yet, the longer-term effect remained—hostility, anxiety, and a desire for vengeance. In some cases, these concerns came to dominate the children's development.

Children of Alcoholics

Another specific body of literature that bears examination is that related to children of alcoholics. The importance of this population does not stem entirely from the common assumption that alcohol abuse and wife abuse are highly correlated but also from the similarity in symptomatology between children exposed to wife abuse and children of alcoholics.

Alcoholism in the family can affect a child in a number of ways. Despite the many different theoretical frameworks (e.g., biological versus stress) that have been used to explain alcoholism, there is some consensus among theorists that children raised in alcoholic families may be at risk for developing adjustment difficulties (West & Prinz, 1987). In addition to acting-out behaviors and difficulties at school, more subtle differences have also been described. For example, feelings and attitudes may develop whereby children may learn to be very hard on themselves and take responsibility for things that were not their fault. The child may have difficulty concentrating in school as a result of being preoccupied with thinking about what is happening at home. Children of alcoholics have also been described as having the following characteristics: confusion, shame, anger, guilt, fear, helplessness, and isolation. Children of alcoholics may have feelings of responsibility for their parents or for stopping their parents from drinking, similarly to how children exposed to wife abuse try to prevent their father from assaulting their mother. The two populations thus share a sense of responsibility for causing the parental behavior of drinking or assaulting.

Children of Parents with Psychiatric Disorders

The issues relating to children with a psychiatrically disordered parent are also of specific interest to those working with battered women and their children. While no evidence to date has suggested that women with a psychiatric illness are more likely to be assaulted by their partners, there is some suggestion that battered women may develop or present some psychiatric symptoms following their victimization. Of further concern are the battered women who have appeared in mental health facilities and have been misdiagnosed as schizophrenic or paranoid (Rosewater, 1984). There is growing evidence to suggest that children of parents with psychiatric disorders are at risk for their own future development (Factor & Wolfe, in press). In particular, children of schizophrenic and depressed mothers have been shown to have more difficulties in their social adjustment than children with well-adjusted parents (Weintraub, Liebert, & Neale, 1978; Weintraub, Prinz, & Neale, 1975). Psychologically disturbed parents may provide poor models for their children and lack consistent and effective family management skills.

It is interesting that Rutter (1971) found that discord in intact families was of more significance in predicting antisocial behavior of children than was the psychiatric illness of a parent. Thus, when the marriage was harmonious, there was no perceptible increase in antisocial behavior associated with parental personality disturbance. Similarly, Emery (1982) found that marital discord accounted for most of the variance in explaining children's disturbed school behavior among children with parents who were suffering from unipolar depression or bipolar disorder. (When the parental diagnosis was schizophrenia, however, marital discord did not explain the children's problems in school.)

POSTTRAUMATIC STRESS DISORDER

As illustrated in the previous chapters, the trauma of being exposed to marital violence makes children more vulnerable to a variety of serious symptomatic behaviors. Clinical and empirical data presented throughout this volume suggest that children exposed to wife abuse may be similar to those children described as suffering from posttraumatic stress disorder (PTSD). PTSD is classified as a type of anxiety disorder by the American Psychiatric Association (1987). The disorder may have an onset at any age following exposure to a psychologically traumatic event that is generally outside the range of usual human experience. Diagnostic criteria for PTSD include the following: (a) existence of a recognizable stressor that would evoke significant symptoms of distress in almost everyone; (b) reexperiencing of the trauma as evidenced by at least one of the following – recurrent and intrusive recollections of the event, recurrent dreams of the event, sudden acting or feeling as if the traumatic event were recurring because of an association with an environmental or ideational stimulus; (c) numbing of responsiveness to or reduced involvement with the external world, beginning some time after the trauma, as shown by at least one of the following – markedly diminished interest in one or more significant activities, feeling of detachment or estrangement from others, constricted affect; and (d) at least two of the following symptoms that were not present before the trauma – hyperalertness or exaggerated startle response, sleep disturbance, guilt about surviving when others have not or about behavior required for survival, memory impairment or trouble concentrating, avoidance of activities that arouse recollection of the traumatic event, intensification of symptoms by exposure to events that symbolize or resemble the traumatic event (American Psychiatric Association, 1987, p. 238).

The applicability of the PTSD disorder to children's exposure to family violence is straightforward. Evidence presented throughout this volume suggests that many of the reactions of children can be classified as "trauma responses," most notably their proclivity to explosive bursts of anger and aggression, their fixation on the trauma and reduction of normal, routine activities, and somatic and emotional complaints. Because the emotional development of children is intimately connected with the safety and nurturance provided by their family environment, they suffer a loss of faith that there is order and continuity in life (Van der Kolk, 1987). Even more damaging is the concern that the family itself plays the most crucial role in protecting the child from traumatization and assisting in his or her recovery. Thus the notion of posttraumatic stress implies that children who chronically witness wife abuse in their homes may display emotional symptomatology at some point in time that may be quite far removed from the initial traumatic events. Furthermore, such symptoms may not be readily detectable as being PTSD-related, because they may be expressed in a manner that disguises their origin and etiology (consider, for example, juvenile violence, running away from home, and extreme oppositional behavior).

CHILDREN'S PROTECTIVE FACTORS

Not all children exposed to wife abuse display elevated symptoms of maladaptive coping and distress. Although approximately one-third of the boys and one-fifth of the girls in shelters were found to have symptoms falling in the clinical range, a significant proportion of the remaining children were showing fewer negative symptoms and even above-average strengths in social competence and adjustment (Wolfe et al., 1985).

Researchers have begun to investigate factors that may account for the resilience seen in some of these children. A clinical and research consensus is forming in favor of viewing children's coping mechanisms as being influenced by more than one factor. In a review of the stressors of childhood, Garmezy (1983) found that the protective factors of the children could be divided into three categories: (a) dispositional attributes of the child (e.g., ability to adjust to new situations); (b) support within the family system (e.g., good relationship with one parent); and (c) support figures outside the family system (e.g., peers, relatives).

In a review of studies looking at children from discordant families, Emery (1982) suggested that a particularly warm relationship with one parent can mitigate, but not eliminate, the effects of marital turmoil on children. Similarly, in a study investigating the postdivorce adjustment of 411 children, Pett (1982) found that the most important predictor of a child's social adjustment was the quality of the custodial parent's relationship with the child. He divided his sample of children from discordant families into two groups—those who had a good relationship with one parent (defined in terms of absence of severe criticism and presence of high warmth) and those who did not have a good relationship with either parent. He found that a good relationship served to provide a buffering effect, and among the children with a good relationship, only 25% showed a conduct disorder (compared with 75% of those lacking such a relationship).

There has also been research conducted that has examined the role of children's social supports outside of the family. For example, Rae-Grant et al. (1984) surveyed 2,435 randomly chosen children (aged 6 to 12) and their families to obtain unbiased estimates of the prevalence of four psychiatric disorders (conduct disorder, neurosis, hyperactivity, and somatization). They found that the presence of protective factors such as friendships with peers, participating in activities outside school, competence in sports and other activities, and good school performance could distinguish between those children who were diagnosed as having a behavior disorder and those who were diagnosed as not having a behavior disorder.

Sandler (1980) also investigated the hypothesis that social support moderates the effects of stress on children. Using 99 children from kindergarten to grade three, Sandler measured life stress, child adjustment, and the presence or absence of three resources of social support: one-parent or two-parent family, older sibling versus no older sibling, and ethnic congruity with the community. He found that older siblings and two-parent families were support resources that moderated the effects of stress on young, economically poor children. Apparently, therefore, good relationships with peers or with other adults outside the family can serve to mitigate the effects of stress (Rutter, 1983).

There is further evidence that children's coping reactions can vary as a function of their developmental stage (Hetherington, 1979). Research with preschool children has demonstrated that disruptions in their normal family functioning is associated with maladaptive behaviors both in the home and in other social situations (Hess & Camara, 1979; Wallerstein & Kelly, 1975). Similarly, Kurdek (1981) suggests that young children are generally less adjusted than older children as a result of the dependence of the younger children on their caregivers and the younger children's lack of sufficient cognitive development to allow them to interpret surrounding events accurately. While family disruption certainly has a negative influence on older children's social interactions, it has been suggested (Hetherington, 1979; Kurdek, 1981) that they are better able to cope with the stress because of their use of peers and schools as sources of information, satisfaction, and support. Although children of different ages react to different aspects of divorce (e.g., younger children are concerned that they will be abandoned by the second parent, while older children are more likely to view their father's absence as a sign of rejection), it does not follow necessarily that one group of children is more strongly affected than another (Wallerstein, 1983).

To consider children's abilities to cope with divorce, Wallerstein (1983) conducted a 10-year study of 60 divorcing families. In her report, she outlines interrelated coping tasks (e.g., resolving anger and self-blame, disengaging from parental conflict and distress, and resuming customary pursuits) that she suggests children must be able to resolve in order to achieve a sense of independence and an ability to maintain a trusting and loving relationship. While acknowledging the influence of the many factors within the family that affect the child's adjustment (e.g., unresolved conflict, support of child), Wallerstein suggests that the child's ability to master the necessary coping tasks is the single most important factor in his or her adjustment.

There are several limitations inherent in research conducted on the variables presumed to moderate children's stress and coping that deserve mention. One issue involves the rating of the strength of the tie. One buffer may provide a much greater effect than another, yet many of the analyses that have been conducted have treated all moderators as equal in strength (Wellman, 1981). Further, assessing moderators involves the multidimensional nature of individual social relationships. For example, it is possible that not all of the identified moderators are necessarily positive or that one moderator may be a source of stress in one event and a support in another (Eckenrode & Gore, 1981; Wellman, 1981). This promising research direction will likely produce new insights and clarification in coming years.

SUMMARY

This chapter has provided an understanding of how witnessing wife assault affects children. A theoretical framework was presented to clarify how wife assault has an impact on children directly through exposure to aggressive models and indirectly through the stress created for the mother. In the latter part of the chapter, this impact was compared with other overwhelming life experiences; the posttraumatic stress disorder was considered as a unifying concept; and the importance of protective factors in child adjustment was outlined. Chapter 4 will attempt to translate this framework and research findings into the development of assessment and intervention strategies for children of battered women.

4

ISSUES IN ASSESSMENT AND INTERVENTION STRATEGIES

Children of battered women present a special challenge to mental health professionals and researchers who try to understand what has happened to these children and what impact these events have had. In some circumstances, such as admission to a shelter, there may be many sources of information (victim, police, emergency room physicians) to describe the violent episode and its immediate consequences. In other circumstances, the violence may be undetected, but alert teachers and social workers may have strong suspicions based on children's behavior and their unusual reactions to normal events (e.g., resisting a return home after school ends on a Friday afternoon). These assessment issues require discussion from the perspective of measurement, differential diagnosis, and disclosure of violence in the home.

MEASUREMENT OF FAMILY VIOLENCE AND CHILD ADJUSTMENT

Measuring violence in the family is a source of considerable debate in an area that has only recently received significant attention from researchers. The current yardstick in the field is the Conflict Tactics Scale (CTS), which was developed by Straus and his colleagues as part of a major survey of violence in American families (Straus et al., 1980). This measure focuses on the frequency of specific behaviors by spouses in their interactions with each other and their children. The behaviors are divided into three major categories: verbal reasoning (e.g., discussed the issues calmly), verbal aggression (e.g., did or said something to spite the other one), and violence (e.g., kicked, bit, or hit with a fist).

Although the CTS was developed to identify the realistic incidence of violent acts in families without regard to actual injuries (Gelles & Straus, 1988), this asset is also seen as a liability by some researchers. That is, less severe acts may result in serious injuries (e.g., a shove or push at the top of a flight of stairs), and more severe acts may not cause any *physical* injuries (e.g., firing a gun that misses the intended target). Aside from this problem there is also concern about the reliability of a victim's recall, especially of repeated acts in which the batterer may tend to minimize the events and the victim may exaggerate her own responses of self-defense (Dutton, 1988). In spite of these concerns, no other researchers have developed an alternative measure that has widespread utilization. A decade of research with the CTS will continue to be the comparative basis for new measures.

Another measurement problem concerns the definition of *witnessing violence.* Although children may observe a wide range of verbal and physical abuse, their observations may vary according to the time and place of the violence. Children may be physically present and observe the violence directly. They may be in their rooms asleep and awaken to overhear part of a violent episode. Children may not see or hear anything at the time of the violence but return from school to see the consequences in terms of physical injuries and visible bruises. In our own research and clinical practice, we have found little reliability between children's reports of their observations and parents' knowledge of what the children know. We have discovered that it is important to interview both children and mothers to elicit their observations and roles in violent incidents. In addition, children and mothers need to clarify a history of multiple partners and repeated victimization. Children may have witnessed a broad range of violent behavior from the father and stepfather or other adult males in the home across various periods of time. The problem in measurement reflects the complex reality of what behaviors these children have been exposed to during many years. Isolated, discrete events are the exception rather than the rule.

Stullman, Schoenenberger, and Hanks (1987) have discussed the importance of assessing the impact of violence on children within the context of other family variables. They stress an understanding of the "psychological climate" of a family in terms of types and range of emotions as well as the psychological functioning of caretakers (such as the ability to protect the children). They have outlined a typology of violence and family functioning that is informative, yet it too goes beyond psychometric measurement.

The challenge of defining *traumatic events* is matched by the search for comprehensive measures of the impact of these events on children. Most research programs and mental health centers rely on broad-based reports of child adjustment, such as that provided by the Child Behavior Checklist (CBCL) (Achenbach & Edelbrock, 1983). This latter measure has been utilized by our research team (e.g., Wolfe et al., 1986) and other investigators in this field (e.g., Hughes, 1982) because the adjustment problems of these children described by shelter staff and clinical observation can be well conceptualized by the CBCL's internalizing and externalizing behavior problem scales and in social competence scales.

The CBCL and other collateral reports of children's adjustment need to be complemented by direct interviews with children and observations by other significant adults in each child's life, such as his or her teacher. Relying on a mother's report alone may be problematic because of her high level of distress and distorted perceptions associated with shelter admission or chronic violence (Hughes, 1988). For example, reports of a significant interaction between maternal depression and children's noncompliance has been demonstrated, indicating that more negative reports of child adjustment are made when mothers are experiencing their own emotional problems (Brody & Forehand, 1986). This latter study describes the very combination of parent-child characteristics that often faces many battered women. Going one step further, Emery and O'Leary (1982) hypothesized that a gender bias may influence mothers to make more negative reports of their son's adjustment after being abused by fathers, whereas reports on daughter's adjustment are less influenced in this way.

Although the CBCL provides an overview of children's adjustment problems and their severity in comparison with clinical and normal populations, it does not claim to replace the rich, qualitative information available directly from the children. This information is essential to any differential diagnosis. Externalizing behavior problems may relate to any one of a number of factors associated with conduct disorder and antisocial behavior (Kazdin, 1987). Internalizing behavior and emotional adjustment problems may indicate exposure to one or more traumatic life events that produce the posttraumatic stress disorder outlined in Chapter 3. Interviews with children of battered women often provide a wealth of information about traumatic events and children's perceptions of each parent's role in the violence. The interview may be an important starting point in developing intervention strategies by assessing the child's level of denial and present coping style. The interview may need to be well structured, in part to discuss specific problem areas that have been identified previously (e.g., subtle symptoms). These areas include the child's attitudes and responses to violence, sense of responsibility for the violence, and knowledge and skills in dealing with violent incidents. To guide us in our clinical research interview, we utilized the format outlined in Figure 4.1 with children over age 6.

The Child Witness to Violence Interview has provided valuable additional information about children who experience these traumatic events. The interview enables us to explore more subtle symptoms that children do not reveal with other assessment techniques. The results of the interview offer some insights about the children's perceptions of violence within the family as well as in a broader context in the popular images they choose from television violence.

In assessing the validity of the Child Witness to Violence Interview, we compared 28 children in shelters with a matched group of 28 children who were similar in age, sex distribution, number of siblings, and family income. Children who witnessed violence in their families had significantly more inappropriate responses to attitudes about anger and less knowledge about basic safety skills (Jaffe, Wilson, & Wolfe, 1989). We have also found some evidence of a "double dose" effect (Heath et al., 1986), which hypothesizes an interaction of the impact of parental violence and high levels of television violence. In one study, children exposed to higher levels of television violence and wife abuse had the most inappropriate responses to the interview questions on attitudes about anger (Girardin, 1988).

DISCLOSURE OF VIOLENCE

Most children are protective of their parents and hesitant to disclose the violence that goes on "behind closed doors" in their home. Children are most likely to share their observations at the time of crisis such as a police intervention, an admission to a shelter, or in extreme trauma, such as witnessing their mother's death. Interviewers must deal with the child's obvious confusion and highly charged emotions in these situations but not pressure a child to offer more than he or she is capable of expressing. Initial decisions about police and court processes are essential to avoid further traumatizing the child by repeated interviews with strangers (Goodman & Rosenberg, 1987). Referrals for ongoing counseling are important to protect the child from reaching out and finding no available follow-through. The consequences of disclosure of severe violence with no treatment may lead to later denial and serious mental health difficulties (Pynoos & Eth, 1984).

Disclosure may be inadvertent through spontaneous utterances or reactions to classroom material or discussions. Predisclosure may only consist of adjustment problems that are waiting for direct questions regarding

A. ATTITUDES & RESPONSES TO ANGER

What kinds of things make you really mad?

Have you ever felt really mad at someone in your family? When? What did you do?

When you're really mad at something or someone, do you ever:
(Circle: 0 = Never; 1 = Sometimes; 2 = Often)

a)	yell, scream, swear	0	1	2
b)	fight, hit, punch	0	1	2
c)	talk to someone	0	1	2
d)	walk away	0	1	2
e)	go to room	0	1	2
f)	other	0	1	2

If someone your own age teases you, what do you usually do?

Do you also:

a) ignore them ____
b) ask them to stop ____
c) tell someone ____
d) threaten them ____
e) hit them ____
f) other ____

If someone your own age takes something without asking, what do you usually do?

Do you also:

a) ignore them ____
b) ask them to stop ____
c) tell someone ____
d) threaten them ____
e) hit them ____
f) other ____

If someone your own age hits you, what do you usually do?

Do you also:

a) ignore them ____
b) ask them to stop ____
c) tell someone ____
d) threaten them ____
e) hit them ____
f) other ____

If your mom or dad does something that you don't like, what do you do?

If an adult other than your parent does something that you don't like, what do you do?

What do you think is the best way to deal with something when you're really mad?

What are your three favourite TV shows?

Of all the characters you have seen on TV, in movies, sports, or music, who would you most like to be? Why?

Figure 4.1. The Children Witness to Violence Interview

How does it make you feel to hear them fight about you?

a) scared ____
b) sad ____
c) mad ____
d) confused ____
e) other ____

Do you think you could have ever done anything to prevent mom and dad from fighting? If yes, what.

C. SAFETY SKILLS

What do you do if mom and dad are arguing?

Do you ever:

a) stay in the same room ____
b) leave/hide ____
c) phone someone ____
d) run out/get someone ____
e) do to older sibling ____
f) ask parents to stop ____
g) act out ____
h) other ____

Can you tell when arguing will lead to dad hitting mom? How?

Can you tell when arguing will lead to mom hitting dad? How?

What do you do if dad is hitting mom when you are in the same room?

Do you ever:

a) stay in the same room ____
b) leave/hide ____
c) phone someone ____
d) run out/get someone ____
e) do to older sibling ____
f) ask parents to stop ____
g) act out ____
h) other ____

What do you do if dad is hitting mom when you are in a different room?

Do you ever:

a) stay in the same room ____
b) leave/hide ____
c) phone someone ____
d) run out/get someone ____
e) do to older sibling ____
f) ask parents to stop ____
g) act out ____
h) other ____

If you were hit by mom or dad, what would you do or what have you done?

Do you ever:

a) stay in the same room ____
b) leave/hide ____
c) phone someone ____
d) run out/get someone ____
e) do to older sibling ____
f) ask parents to stop ____
g) act out ____
h) other ____

What do you do if mom or dad are hitting your brother or sister?

Have you ever told anybody about this?

In an emergency (ie. danger to mom/self) who would you call?

Their phone number is: ____________

What would you say?

Figure 4.1 (continued)

How often do people in the same family hit each other?

Never Sometimes A Lot

How often do strangers hit each other?

Never Sometimes A Lot

Do you think it's alright for a man to hit a woman? (Why/why not)

(Elicit from child any conditions in which hitting is acceptable)

a) stays out late ___
b) house is messy ___
c) doesn't do as told ___
d) drinking ___
e) self-defense ___
f) other ___

Do you think it's alright for a woman to hit a man? (Why/why not)

(Elicit from child any conditions in which hitting is acceptable)

a) stays out late ___
b) house is messy ___
c) doesn't do as told ___
d) drinking ___
e) self-defense ___
f) other ___

Do you think it's alright for a parent to hit a child? (Why/why not)

(Elicit from child any conditions in which hitting is approved)

a) stays out late ___
b) house is messy ___
c) doesn't do as told ___
d) drinking ___
e) self-defense ___
f) other ___

B. RESPONSIBILITY FOR VIOLENCE

What do you think mom and dad fight about?

Do they also fight about the following things?
(How often? 0 = Never; 1 = Sometimes; 2 = Often)

a) money?	0	1	2
b) job?	0	1	2
c) drinking? (mom; dad)	0	1	2
d) mom or dad seeing someone else?	0	1	2
e) your brothers or sisters?	0	1	2
f) untidy house?	0	1	2
g) other (specify)?	0	1	2
h) you?	0	1	2

Figure 4.1 (continued)

problems in the family. The children we have interviewed are almost universal in their need to be listened to, believed, and supported. They usually are not looking for solutions but an opportunity to share their fears about their mother and perhaps all members of the family. Children at different stages of development may express these feelings directly to adults with whom they feel safe, or indirectly through play and drawings.

In our experience, disclosure will not occur or would be handled poorly if the interviewer fails to acknowledge the child's plight or offers the child unrealistic solutions to end the nightmare. Questions about the violence they have witnessed must indicate that the adult understands that the child is not alone in experiencing this trauma. While it is important not to minimize the trauma experienced, it is also necessary to communicate in a nonjudgmental manner to the child that violence occurs in other families. Children often believe that other people will think less of them because of their father's behavior, and they need reassurance that they are not alone in this regard.

Adults must develop a positive relationship with a child before he or she will offer more information beyond the initial disclosure. Children may need to give bits of family secrets at several different interviews before an adult feels that they have given a complete picture. Children may need to consider how they will eventually cope with the consequences of violence more effectively and how to allow the adult who receives the disclosure to contact their mother and involve appropriate community resources (of course, action has to be expedited when children disclose possibly lethal or highly dangerous situations). Despite an adult's well-intended tendency and desire to encourage children and adolescents to "talk about how they are feeling," many children will not be prepared to do so right away. Questioning the child on different occasions to express how he or she feels may result in feelings of pressure and discomfort and may be counterproductive in eliciting the intended emotions. Therefore, while recognizing the importance of children's self-expression, counselors and other care providers are well advised to spend as much time as necessary to permit the child to develop a level of comfort that will facilitate his or her emotional expression and release.

CONCEPTUALIZING GOALS FOR INTERVENTION

The assessment of children who witness violence in their family should lead to the development of an intervention strategy. This strategy has to consider many factors in regard to the extent of the violence, the impact on the child's behavioral and emotional adjustment, and the functioning of each parent. First and foremost, intervention has to be centered on the issue of safety. Children who live with ongoing violence need to be protected from the direct and indirect consequences of this violence. Children who continue not to feel safe in their home will not be able to focus on loftier goals of behavioral and emotional changes.

Beyond safety, many mental health professionals question the value of helping children change when their parents are not prepared to receive appropriate assistance. That is, mothers need to be involved in appropriate individual and group counseling programs, and fathers need to participate in counseling to accept responsibility for their violence. The goal is often not to keep the family together at any cost but to accept the reality that most victims will return to batterers, batterers will find new victims, and children will continue to be exposed to a home environment that may promote the intergenerational transmission of violence (Gentry & Eaddy, 1982).

Obviously, children cannot be denied services when their parents refuse or are unable to take advantage of counseling programs. However, more realistic goals need to be formulated to assist children in coping with ongoing crises. The focus will need to be placed on protection planning for the child (Grusznski et al., 1988) and attenuating the impact of the exposure to violence. This goal represents a challenge analogous to "being sane in insane places" as the child has to avoid responsibility for violence and learn not to imitate repeated aggressive acts.

Different levels of intervention for children can be conceptualized according to primary, secondary, and tertiary prevention programs in reference to the next generation of violent husbands and their victims. Although the research is far from definitive about the intergenerational transmission of violence (Widom, 1989), exposure to wife assault is the single most consistent factor in predicting the behavior of batterers and their victims (Hotaling & Sugarman, 1986). Tertiary intervention programs can be aimed at children in shelters who have been exposed to violence and are already showing serious signs of maladjustment. Secondary intervention programs can be offered to a high-risk group of children who are not yet demonstrating symptoms but are known to have witnessed violence, such as children identified by police officers, family lawyers, and marriage counselors with battered women as clients. Primary prevention programs can be directed at all children and adolescents who are exposed to a number of role models at home, in the community, and in the media that promote violence in intimate relationships. These approaches are explored throughout the remainder of this chapter and in Chapter 5.

CURRENT STRATEGIES FOR HELPING CHILDREN OF BATTERED WOMEN

We tend to prefer the words *strategies* or *intervention* rather than *treatment* because the former terms more accurately capture the developing stage of services for this population. The current efforts of researchers and practitioners represent preliminary attempts to assist a special population of children. It is difficult to articulate clearly an exact treatment regime that can be easily replicated by other clinicians. The definition of effective ingredients of programs, beyond adult attention and reassurance, is speculative at present, and evaluation of programs with well-defined populations and appropriate control groups are possibly another decade away. With this reality in mind, this chapter outlines some promising areas of intervention that merit further investigation and program development.

Crisis Intervention

An optimist would point out that the Chinese symbol for *crisis* is made up of the symbols for *danger* and *opportunity*. Children in crisis genuinely represent both a danger to their physical and mental health and an opportunity for change. The opportunity is the public disclosure of violence to police and shelter staff and a vulnerable emotional state that offers a small opening for skilled professionals.

A vital service that can provide a meaningful crisis intervention for children of battered women is the police. Unfortunately, police officers who provide this service may lack the training, specialized resources, and departmental leadership to address this problem. An example of a successful commitment to this issue is the London (Ontario) Police Force, which was one of the first in North America to hire social work staff to provide crisis consultants for officers and immediate counseling and referrals for family members (Jaffe & Thompson, 1984). This police force was also one of the first in Canada to institute a formal policy on bringing charges in cases of wife assault rather than leaving the onus on the victim to find safety and justice (Jaffe, Wolfe, Telford, & Austin, 1986).

This crisis service provides an attempt to intervene with families when they may be most open to assistance, without blaming the victim for the violence or condoning the behavior of the batterer. The service in London, known as the Family Consultant Service, offers immediate support to the police in handling a complex situation with conflicting needs of family members, especially child witnesses to violence. The consultant staff, members of which are available around the clock, seven days a week, can offer immediate assistance to victims and their children and provide an important bridge to other community agencies.

This program has been the object of several evaluation attempts that have been challenged by a host of factors, including a wide variety of intervention styles and a broad range of clients. However, the preliminary findings are encouraging in terms of police attitudes, coordination of services, and successful referrals to community resources. A three-year follow-up of 379 families who agreed to participate yielded a disappointing response rate of 16%; however, this small but representative sample reported a decrease in verbal aggression and violence and an increase in verbal reasoning as measured by the Conflict Tactics Scale (Jaffe, Finlay, & Wolfe, 1984). Although no separate analyses were done relating specific child problems to violence, there was an overall decrease in emotional and behavioral problems as measured by Quay's Behavior Problem Checklist (Jaffe et al., 1984).

Crisis programs that have been well articulated but not evaluated are offered at many shelters for battered women. These programs have become increasingly focused on the crisis state of the child, the special needs at the time of admission to the shelter, and the development of more extensive programs to assist in recovery. Hughes (1988) has provided an excellent summary of these programs, taking into account the child's age, the child's stage of development, and the history of violence that has been witnessed. In our opinion, many crisis programs at shelters are a tribute to creative thinking because of the limited resources and unknown length of stay that many staff are forced to take into account. When children stay for several weeks and develop trust with shelter staff, more extensive programs like a group counseling approach are possible.

Group Counseling Programs

The most widely suggested intervention for children of battered women is a group counseling program (Grusznski et al., 1988; Hughes, 1988; Wilson, Cameron, Jaffe, & Wolfe, 1989). Most of the group programs described in the literature are housed in shelters for battered women, but they may also involve collaboration with other professionals in child protection or mental health centers (Jaffe, Wilson, & Wolfe, 1986). These programs are usually targeted at school-age children between the ages of 8 and 13 years, because they are most open to this approach and constitute a large percentage of shelter residents.

Although most children will require a great deal of individual attention from shelter staff and other professionals at the time of crisis, group programs represent an essential follow-through service for these children. Groups allow children an opportunity to learn that they are not alone in dealing with their trauma and that other children have comparable life experiences. Children can learn helpful coping strategies from other "survivors" and caring adults who lead the group. For many children this intervention represents their first opportunity to discuss the issue of violence in their family. They are often anxious to share their thoughts and feelings and sometimes surprised to find alternative ideas on conflict resolution.

The group model we have utilized in our research and program development is based partly on the model suggested by Alessi and Hearn (1984) for children in shelters in the Buffalo, New York, area. Essentially, the group deals with the most important areas of emotional, behavioral, and cognitive problems associated with witnessing wife assault. We try to address children's adjustment difficulties as well as the more subtle symptoms related to attitudes about violence and responsibility for adult behavior.

We have been involved in developing groups in five different communities in southwestern Ontario. We have encouraged a close collaboration between shelters and other community resources by working with male and female cotherapists (group leaders) from different agencies. Many of the children are former residents of shelters or referrals from children's mental health facilities or child protection agencies. The children are divided into programs for 8- to 10-year-olds and 11- to 13-year-olds. The framework consists of 10 weekly sessions of approximately 1 1/2 hours each. We have worked with a structured format, although the special issues for individual children and ongoing crises demand great flexibility. The issues we address in the 10 sessions include the following:

(1)Introduction. This is a review of the purpose of the group, which is to help children cope with traumatic events and learn that they have had experiences similar to their peers. Throughout the program, some children may disclose their victimization involving sexual and/or physical abuse and need to know the limits of confidentiality that result from the legislated reporting responsibility of group leaders.

(2)Labeling feelings. Children must learn how to express the many feelings they have had in reaction to the violence they have witnessed. Many of their emotions may create conflict and confusion in themselves, and they need an opportunity to discuss the fear, anger, sadness, and sense of isolation they have experienced.

(3) Dealing with anger. Anger is a major area of concern for those children because they need to learn that it is okay to be angry, but it is not okay to hit. The group can be aided, through a number of exercises, to consider and practice healthy alternatives in expressing anger.

(4) Safety skills. Children spend a great deal of time worrying about future violent episodes. They need to plan ways to protect themselves and seek assistance in emergency situations.

(5) Social support. Isolation has been a family style for many children. They need to learn that they are part of a large community with important resources that include friends, extended family, neighbors, and appropriate agencies. Each child must identify and be prepared to utilize a support system for him- or herself.

(6) Social competence and self-concept. Living with violence may produce guilt, shame, and diminished effectiveness at school. Self-esteem is often undermined by the violence in the home. Children need to be encouraged to identify areas of strength and competence and ways that they can feel better about themselves.

(7) Responsibility for parent/violence. Children frequently blame themselves for the violence and seek ways to prevent incidents and protect their mothers. These children need to know that the violence is not their fault. They also must consider that their mother's safety is ultimately a community responsibility and the role of police officers and courts.

(8) Understanding family violence. Children usually maintain several myths about the violence in their family. Mothers are often blamed for their behavior that is seen to bring on the violence. Fathers' behavior may be seen as the fault of alcohol or job stress. Children may be confused by the cycle of violence that makes separation appear inevitable one moment and reconciliation obvious the next moment. They need to learn the facts about violence and be prepared for consistent patterns of behavior.

(9) Wishes about family. Children may express the idea that their lives have been a nightmare and they wish their real parents would come along and rescue them. The children need to resolve their concept of ideal families and the tragic reality around them. In particular, children need an opportunity to discuss their fear and anger about their father's behavior and on the other hand their underlying love for him.

(10) Review and termination. Children need an opportunity to review the material that has been covered in the group and begin the process of terminating close relationships. Some children may have a chance to be in the group again or may find ways to have a group member be part of an ongoing support system.

This model is described in detail elsewhere (Jaffe, Wilson, & Wolfe, 1986; Wilson et al., 1989), and a manual outlining these topics is available. As children attend these sessions they may return home and raise uncomfortable issues for their parents. Therefore, it is important to have group leaders maintain close contact with parents (usually the mother) in order to prepare them for the issues that are covered. Initial information and ongoing feedback to mothers is essential. Some group models suggest that mothers should be part of the group and that parent-child relationships become a major focus.

We have begun to evaluate the impact of our group counseling program and have found some encouraging results (however, no control group has been implemented to date). In one study, 64 children (ages 7 to 13 years, mean age = 10) were assessed in individual interviews before and after receiving the group counseling program. Children completed the structured interview outlined earlier in this chapter as well as the Parent Perception Inventory (Hazzard, Christensen, & Margolin, 1983). Each mother provided relevant background information, indicated the perceptions of changes after the group, and also completed the Child Behavior Checklist (Achenbach & Edelbrock, 1983).

The majority of the mothers (88%) indicated that their children enjoyed the group, and these mothers also perceived a positive change in behavioral adjustment. However, material reported on the Child Behavior Checklist did not support this perception (i.e., there was no significant change in child adjustment problems). The children reported they enjoyed the group themselves and demonstrated a significant change in the area of safety skills in being able to describe more protection strategies in times of emergencies. The children also reported a significant improvement in positive perceptions of each parent. This finding may relate to the group goals of understanding the impact of the violence on their mother and being allowed to separate their feelings of love for their father without having to accept his violent behavior (Jaffe et al., 1989).

Overall, we are finding that the group counseling program is best suited for mild-to-moderate behavior problems in children. For children exposed to repeated acts of severe violence over many years, the group only addressed a small proportion of their numerous concerns. These children required more extensive individual work than the group could provide. Our analysis is similar to Kazdin's (1987) views of the relative impact of treatment programs for children with conduct disorders of different levels of severity.

Grusznski et al. (1988) recently described the results of a similar group for children of battered women. This group covered many of the topics previously outlined and was augmented by additional services for the mother and children. Group leaders completed clinical ratings on 371 children who attended the program during a four-year period. Results indicated that children were able to improve their self-concept, understand that violence in the home was not their fault, become more aware of protection planning, and learn new ways of resolving conflict without resorting to violence. As with our own studies, no control group comparison was available to examine the extent to which children might demonstrate these improvements over time by themselves or with some adult attention. In comparison, group activities focused less on violence in the home than was true of our group. Nonetheless, these studies are encouraging to those researchers and practitioners seeking the most promising intervention strategies to pursue.

PRIMARY PREVENTION PROGRAMS

Professionals in the field of family violence consistently stress the importance of primary prevention programs to change the underlying attitudes and behaviors that condone and promote violence between family members. Several authors have suggested that school systems could be a valuable partner in community efforts to raise awareness about violence in intimate relationships and teach alternative forms of conflict resolution.

Several projects have been developed in school systems to address this issue. The most advanced efforts have been developed by the Coalition for Battered Women in Southern California (Levy, 1984) and in Minnesota (Stavrou-Petersen & Gamache, 1988). In both cases, shelters for battered women and parallel services for batterers and children have combined their expertise to design learning material for children of different ages to promote "skills for violence-free relationships" (Levy, 1984).

The Minnesota program has received the most comprehensive evaluation to date. This program stresses the importance of having teachers fully trained to utilize new curriculum material and to offer instruction on a consistent basis across schools. In pretesting, using several questions on attitudes and knowledge about violence, the evaluation team discovered a high incidence of dating violence reported by girls and boys (34% and 15%, respectively) and traditional sex differences on the roles of men and women (e.g., given the statement, "In serious relationships between men and women, men should be the leaders and decision makers," only 58% of the boys disagreed while 94.4% of the girls disagreed).

At 12 junior (grades 7-9) and senior (grades 10-12) high schools across urban and rural communities, 688 students received the curriculum material and were compared at posttest to 496 students matched for grades and school area who did not receive this instruction. Although no significant differences were found in attitudes about violence, encouraging findings were outlined in regard to knowledge about family violence issues. Senior high students were able to identify more resources to contact for victims and assailants in violent families (Jones, 1987).

Primary prevention programs aimed at large groups of adolescents seem ideal from two perspectives. First, adolescents are anxious to grow independent from their families and usually develop their first intimate relationships outside the home. Some of these early relationships are already abusive. For example, Jones (1987) found a 34% incidence of physical abuse in the teenage girls she surveyed. Likewise, Mercer (1987) found an 11% incidence of physical abuse, 17% of verbal abuse, and 20% of sexual abuse in a survey of 217 young women, ages 16 to 20, in Toronto-area high schools. Clearly, the issue of violence in relationships is highly relevant for this population in terms of potential violence, batterers, and a peer group that needs to challenge this behavior.

A second perspective on these prevention programs is the possibility of reaching adolescents who have witnessed their mothers being assaulted, without singling them out in a school system. Advertising special groups for child witnesses of violence in a school system may threaten guilty parents and make adolescents feel that they have been labeled. Providing a broad-based program for all students will address, in part, the needs of those students. In Jones's (1987) evaluation of the Minnesota program, she reported that 25% of the girls and 17.8% of the boys had witnessed violence between their parents. Moreover, these students reported more violence in dating relationships than those students living in violence-free homes. The school curriculum obviously has special relevance for these students, although no separate analyses were presented to indicate any differential impact of the program.

EXISTING TREATMENT PROGRAMS APPLIED TO THIS SPECIAL POPULATION

In our work with children of battered women, we have been wary of not "reinventing the wheel" with new intervention programs when many existing treatment strategies could be applied to this population. Although these children have some special needs that may be unique to their traumatic experience, most of their presenting problems have been the subject of considerable clinical research. The biggest obstacle that we have found is professionals not being aware of violence in the family and not asking the basic questions. All too often, health and social service professionals will be struggling with treating symptoms of aggression and withdrawal without understanding the home environment that has given rise to them.

Any treatment program for these children starts with accurate information about the home environment. An example about improving this first step is increasing awareness in physicians and nurses in the health care system. Klingbeil and Boyd (1984) have pointed out that a crucial frontline health care facility is often the hospital emergency room, which traditionally has overlooked the victimization of battered women and their children. These authors have suggested the development of specific abuse protocols that include implications of wife abuse for children. Klingbeil and Boyd (1984, p. 25) clearly summarized the importance of this process:

> What can emergency room personnel do about domestic violence? Probably the most significant contribution any member of the health care industry can provide is the initial, accurate, and primary diagnosis that domestic violence has occurred. To comply with the victim's attempts to hide the phenomenon is to compound the problem. We found that a frank, straightforward approach, with all staff making direct inquiries in suspected cases, has proved invaluable. Many patients expressed great relief when health care providers directly acknowledged the fact of domestic violence.

Whether or not family violence is accurately assessed, many children will reflect its existence in their behavior and thereby draw attention to themselves and the family. Of all the symptoms receiving attention, none gets a more immediate response from parents and professionals than conduct disorders or antisocial behavior. The wide diversity of behaviors assumed under this diagnosis may include hitting others, stealing, destroying other people's property, being disruptive and disrespectful at school, and running away. Kazdin (1987) has identified the most "promising" treatment programs for this diagnosis in children of battered women. Parent management training appears to be one of these treatments that has been supported by a great deal of systematic clinical research. It is interesting to note that these programs directed at making parents more effective in their discipline of children may have a positive side effect of decreasing maternal depression as well (Kazdin, 1987). This finding supports the work of many shelters that direct their efforts to making an overwhelmed victim of violence regain some sense of self-esteem and mastery in dealing with her children (Hughes, 1986).

Kazdin (1987) also recommends the approach of Alexander and his colleagues, who utilize functional family therapy, mainly with delinquent children involved in the court system. The approach involves changing existing interaction patterns in families in order to foster better communication and support among family members (Alexander & Parsons, 1982). Before this program can be utilized with violent families, treatment professionals need to ensure basic safety for battered women and their children and protect against batterers using this approach to justify their behavior and blame the victim. One could hypothesize that this approach may be very helpful in dealing with children of battered women who tend to accept roles and responsibilities beyond appropriate boundaries in their family.

Another treatment strategy that has a less extensive empirical basis but is well connected to research and theory of child development is cognitive-problem-solving skills training (Kazdin, 1987; Kendall & Braswell, 1985). This strategy addresses some of the very central adjustment problems in boys who witness violence in the home. An attempt is made to assist these youngsters in gaining better behavioral self-control by being aware of the consequences of their behavior and practicing alternative strategies to impulsive and aggressive acts. Based on the work of Rosenberg (1984), who found deficits in problem-solving skills in this population, this approach seems very timely for children exposed to violence. This program could be an essential strategy for all children who remain in a shelter long enough to build new areas of social competencies.

At the other end of the spectrum from conduct disorders and behavior excesses are behavior deficits defined by withdrawal, anxiety, and depression. Current treatment strategies in this area are varied but increasing recognition is being given to the consequences of traumatic events and posttraumatic stress disorders. Van der Kolk (1987) recognizes the impact of overwhelming life experiences on children and points out that a major focus of treatment relates to children regaining some sense of mastery in their lives. He indicates the specific challenge of treating clients who may be alternating between numbing emotions and intrusive thoughts, and suggests patience and preparation in therapists to deal with these fluctuations.

Vulnerability to later stressful events and the need for treatment are indicated by the number of children who experience different forms of violence without treatment and end up with the psychiatric labels of *borderline personality* and *multiple personality* (Van der Kolk, 1987). The compounding factor for these children is that they experience or witness violence from the very adults they trust and depend on for safety and nurturance (Krugman, 1987).

One promising treatment strategy for the problem of posttraumatic stress disorder is outlined by Flannery (1987). He suggests a stress management approach that is based in part on Seligman's model of learned helplessness (Seligman, 1975). Although there is a lack of empirical support for this approach with children, it seems to match the previously discussed needs of children who witness violence. These children need to feel some sense of safety and mastery over overwhelming emotions of fear and confusion. Experiencing relaxation through behavior and cognitive exercises to deal with intrusive thoughts and emotions is essential. Developing protection plans and knowledge of a support system may reduce stress and prepare for future crises. Several of these ingredients are already being utilized in group counseling programs for children in shelters for battered women (Grusznski et al., 1988; Wilson et al., 1989).

SUMMARY

Children who witness violence in their family have many needs that must be addressed by mental health and social service professionals. The first step in developing an intervention strategy for this population is a proper assessment of these children and the impact of the traumatic events they have experienced. This chapter included a structured interview that we utilize in identifying subtle symptoms in these children related to attitudes about violence, responsibility for adult behavior, and safety planning. This interview could complement existing strategies, including standardized behavior checklists completed by parents and teachers.

The chapter also identified some promising intervention strategies for these children, including crisis services, group counseling programs, and school-based primary prevention programs. It is also important to consider existing child treatment programs that could be applied to child witnesses who demonstrate externalizing and internalizing behavioral and emotional adjustment problems. Although programs directed at children who witness violence are in their infancy, the possibilities that have been raised are encouraging. The next, concluding chapter suggests the many implications of existing knowledge about these children for community services—including the social service, mental health, justice, and education systems.

5

IMPLICATIONS FOR CHILDREN'S SERVICES

The previous chapter addressed current assessment and intervention strategies for children of battered women. This chapter will focus on how these strategies can be applied to particular target groups.

An increasing awareness of the special needs of children who witness violence has led to some innovative programs aimed at their emotional and behavioral adjustment problems. Social service, mental health, and justice systems have had to examine their existing policies, procedures, and services offered to battered women and their children, and to become more responsive to this population's special needs. If the 1970s and 1980s were a period of ending the silence and secrecy about physical and emotional abuse, it can be anticipated that the 1990s will be a time when highly specialized programs will be developed and traditional agencies will be challenged on how they are responding to the issue of family violence. Throughout this chapter we will examine some major trends in the delivery of services to children of battered women, including programs in shelters, child protection services, children's mental health centers, courts, and the school system.

CHILDREN'S PROGRAMS IN SHELTERS

Shelters for battered women have undergone a phenomenal period of growth throughout North America. In Canada alone, the number of shelters receiving public funding has gone from 71 to over 300 in the past 10 years (MacLeod, 1989). However, only recently have shelters begun to examine the level of services for children who accompany their mothers.

Shelter staff have always been aware of the nature of emotional and behavioral problems that child witnesses to violence may exhibit. As mentioned in Chapter 1, the documentation of this trauma by shelter staff played a significant role in highlighting the need for more intensive community interventions. The issue has been one of funding and mandate. Shelters developed on shoestring budgets (many still exist in this manner) with dedicated staff and volunteers who struggled to deal with women and children in crisis. Even as funding improved, concern existed that new dollars for children's programs would not be possible and, in fact, would fragment the limited funds that were available (MacLeod, 1987). Nevertheless, a significant focus has now been placed on these children, and the majority of battered women who seek shelter bring children with them. On average, for every battered woman in a shelter there are two children who also require a high level of specialized services (Carlson, 1984). Surveys of shelters in the past decade revealed a paucity of these programs. For example, in one Canadian survey, only one-third of the shelters were able to provide child-care staff for this population and only one-quarter could offer any counseling beyond parent relief and recreation (McKay, 1981). The same problem was documented in the United States in the early 1980s (Carlson, 1984).

Recently, the growing recognition of the needs of these children, coupled with greater public awareness and funding, has resulted in more shelters developing special services for children (e.g., Armstrong, 1986; Alessi & Hearn, 1984; Grusznski et al., 1988; Hughes, 1982; Woods, 1981). Some jurisdictions have articulated clear policies in this area. For example, the province of Ontario has offered funding to each shelter for child-care staff who act as advocates, counselors, and liaisons with other community agencies. Almost all shelters in the province have taken up this offer and have made the provision of services to children of battered women one of their primary mandates. Rather than competing for other funding or services, this focus appears to complement intervention strategies directed to battered women because their children are most often a major priority on their list of needs (Jaffe & Burris, 1984).

Children's services in shelters usually address a number of issues related to one of the following: the child in crisis, the child-parent (mother) relationship, or the mother's functioning alone. Unquestionably, when women seek refuge after an incident of violence and after years of abuse, their children face an equal crisis and disruption in their lives (Davidson, 1978). A major focus for shelter staff is to ensure the children's needs do not become invisible at this crisis stage. This may represent an ideal opportunity for children to share their feelings and sense some safety and adult support in these circumstances. Children who witness their mother being assaulted are experiencing significant emotional trauma that requires an outlet for expression and some sense of restabilization (Carlson, 1984).

The child-parent relationship becomes a very obvious factor when staff live with mothers and their children on a daily basis. Problematic relationships are the norm because of the violence the children have witnessed as well as the fact that their mother is likely to be emotionally unavailable to them. Children may miss their father and quickly forget or minimize the actual reason why they came to be in the shelter. Accordingly, their mother may be blamed for displacing them from their home and neighborhood friends.

Because some children act out their anxiety, anger, and confusion in disruptive ways, their mothers may have little tolerance or energy to use appropriate child management techniques. Shelter staff may play an important role in mediating between mother and children, clarifying the underlying issues, and preventing reliance on physical punishment and verbal threats as forms of discipline (Armstrong, 1986).

Some shelters may focus primarily on indirect services to children by paying close attention to the battered woman's role as a parent. Through supportive counseling and some parenting relief, the mother is empowered to regain more effective functioning as a parent. Many programs recognize that one-third of the battered women have had few role models for effective parenting because of their own sexual and physical abuse as children. Some clients in a shelter may be unable to function as parents without very specific educational programs to learn new ways of relating to their children (Hughes, 1982).

In most descriptions of children's services in shelters, there is a core of central issues to which staff should be sensitive. Some of these issues may require immediate action by the staff to respond to the child's crisis (e.g., curbs on aggressive behavior, supportive counseling), whereas some issues may be better left for treatment following the crisis (e.g., loss of self-esteem, ambivalence about parental relationship—see Chapter 4). These central issues for shelters include the following:

understanding the child's shock, confusion, anxiety, and distress that exist as a result of the trauma of witnessing violence;

being aware of the child's possible ambivalence about his or her relationship with both parents, including wishes for changes in both mother and father and in their relationship together;

understanding the child's insecurity about his or her future and planning for the mother's next move as well as possible guilt about having caused the violence or not being able to prevent it;

knowing how to deal with the child's aggressive behavior toward mother or other residents;
helping the child to develop a sense of trust and safety in the current environment (Cassady et al., 1987);
helping the child to foster relationships with appropriate nonviolent male models (Armstrong, 1986); and
assisting the child in handling the distress of being removed from familiar environments, such as school, community, and related friends and activities.

In general, these issues relate mostly to the child or adolescent's emotional, cognitive, and behavioral adjustment following a period of family turmoil and disruption. For some children, this period may represent part of an initial crisis, while for other children, the pattern of violent behavior is all too familiar. The challenge for a shelter is to provide a meaningful service on a time-limited basis. Women and children will average only a week at the shelter, and some stay only for one night. Many shelters have developed programs that are directed to specific age groups with specific treatment modalities in mind. Some examples follow:

behavioral techniques to deal with specific problem behaviors, such as aggression in latency-age children (Hughes, 1982);
play assessment and play therapy to encourage preschool children to express feelings about the trauma (Watson, 1986);
engaging adolescents to develop and act out plays about family violence to foster awareness, self-expression, and a sense of helping others (Watson, 1986);
individual counseling for children, including very specific strategies on creating a better understanding of child reaction to current crisis and preparation for future disruptions (Cassady et al. 1987);
structured group counseling for children and adolescents to assist them in gaining peer support and a sense of not being alone with the problem (Alessi & Hearn, 1984); and
multifamily groups that include women and children and are open-ended enough to deal with the reality of a brief, time-limited intervention (these strategies encourage mutual support within and between families in crises; Rhodes & Zelman, 1986).

A vital aspect of shelter services for children is the integration of these programs with other community agencies. Among the most important agencies for this coordinated approach are schools and child protection services.

For many children exposed to violence, school can represent one of two extremes. School is either another environment that produces a sense of failure and frustration or school may be a significant positive and stabilizing factor for the child. After admission to a shelter, a large proportion of children may not attend school because of the fear of the father kidnapping them or they may face the further disruption of a new school environment (Woods, 1981). In any event, this transition is vital for the child as it may represent an opportunity to identify remedial needs, offer individual support, and create some sense of routine and stability.

Shelters may offer a host of school services, including the following:

close liaison with the existing school placement to assure awareness of the trauma and continuity of education (Woods, 1981);

specialized teachers on-site in the shelter to offer remedial assistance and reintegration into the school system after the crisis period (MacLeod, 1987); and

specialized classrooms in schools that have a close relationship with the neighborhood shelter and are prepared for the unique demands on these students (Pepler, Moore, Mae, & Kates, in press) (one innovative model in Toronto, Ontario, involves a school that has integrated the services of the local school board, a shelter, and staff from a near by children's mental health center to maximize the support for child witnesses to wife assault; Pepler et al., in press).

Shelters and child protection agencies have traditionally had a strained relationship (Cummings & Mooney, 1988). Shelter staff advocate for the needs of battered women and are fearful that child protection agencies will revictimize their client (the mother) through apprehension of her children. On the other hand, child protection social workers will advocate for the child not living in a dangerous environment and rule out any consideration of a battered woman returning to her assailant. The reality lies between these polarized positions. Battered women should not be revictimized by child protection services, but children must not be continued to be placed at risk for their physical and emotional well-being.

Shelters that have been effective in working with child protection agencies on behalf of their clients have suggested the following interventions:

training workshops for staff in each agency on the issues surrounding wife assault, including clinical and legal mandates and responsibilities (Cummings & Mooney, 1988);

closer relationships among staff in the two agencies that encourage two-way referrals between the services (Layzer et al., 1985); and

utilizing child protection staff to offer programs such as parenting courses or children's groups in the shelter to help clients see the protection agency's role as acting as "helpers" rather than as only policing abuse (Hughes, 1982).

Clearly, shelters for battered women have emerged as an important service for women and children who are victims of emotional and physical abuse. The programs already developed suggest that children are an important client group that has shaped the design, staffing, and programming of shelters. Future trends will likely include the role of second-stage housing and longer-term programs for children as well as follow-up counseling and support to reach out to those children who do not remain in a shelter long enough to connect with staff at the time of crisis.

DIFFERENTIAL ASSESSMENT AND INTERVENTION STRATEGIES IN CHILDREN'S MENTAL HEALTH CENTERS

Throughout North America, there exists a network of children's mental health centers that have evolved over the past three decades to provide assessment and treatment services for children and adolescents. These services recognize the many adjustment difficulties that children may experience and offer a wide range of residential and nonresidential programs. Through the years, the trend of these programs is to offer community-based rather than institutional interventions, focusing as well on the children within the context of their family, which makes the role of parent and siblings of prime importance. Especially for younger children, intervention strategies have to be founded, as much as possible, on behavioral and cognitive changes in the entire family system.

Obviously, the majority of children and adolescents do not refer themselves to mental health centers. Parents are usually encouraged to make these referrals by school officials or family doctors when children's behavior becomes labeled as "disturbed" or "disturbing." The pattern of children who are referred for assessment and treatment consistently demonstrates several trends. Boys are more likely to be seen as requiring special assistance in comparison with girls, usually by a ratio of as much as 3 or 4 to 1. When boys are referred, the usual adjustment problem is related to aggressive behavior that disrupts the classroom or neighborhood safety. When girls are referred, it is more likely that withdrawal, anxiety, or depression are identified by the referral source. It is interesting to note that the most common referral reasons correspond with the major adjustment problems identified for children of battered women, as outlined in the studies reported in Chapter 3.

Although witnessing violence in the family may account for many symptoms brought to the attention of a children's mental health center, such violence is rarely identified as an issue. Until recently, these centers reflected the same lack of awareness as the rest of society in recognizing the extent of family violence in the community. This lack of awareness may have led to the same misdiagnoses that have been reported for battered women (Jaffe, Wolfe, Wilson, & Zak, 1986). That is, a thorough assessment of children that included psychological testing, extensive family histories, and medical investigations may have overlooked very basic questions about violence in the family. In our experience working with many children's mental health centers, extensive intake information about the child and family never raised the issue of wife assault or the kinds of physical or emotional abuse that children witness in the home. We have seen a positive change in awareness and staff attitudes about the prevalence of the problem by simply including this question on a structured intake form for an agency. Communicating to parents that this problem exists and may relate to childhood adjustment difficulties is a major first step toward successful intervention programs (Carlson, 1984).

There are obviously many steps required beyond asking questions about children's exposure to violence in the home. In one workshop we conducted for a mental health center on this topic, the director was very candid about why this issue was never raised. He indicated:

> "We never ask the question about violence because we would not know what to do about the answer if the parents said yes. . . . what are we supposed to tell the mother and the father and what services are we required to offer the child?"

These are essential questions that children's mental health centers must address. The answers lie in three areas, which are related to staff awareness, networks with other community agencies, and the development of specialized programs or the refocusing of existing ones.

Staff awareness about the issue must be fostered by information about wife assault through workshops and special presentations about violence in the family. Encouraging staff to include questions about violence as part of interviews with children and family members will lead to surprising results. Clients will feel permission to talk about violence and see the problem as a legitimate one that needs to be resolved. Both women and their children may feel that safety and the termination of violence are vital goals that need to be reached before basic adjustment difficulties can be dealt with. Staff will be overwhelmed with the frequency with which clients acknowledge violence in their home.

Staff development on the issue of family violence can be supported and encouraged by case conferences with other agencies. Sharing perspectives on children and their needs with other community professionals such as police officers and shelter staff can be the beginning of a better-integrated response to family violence. For example, the police play a major role in the community as the only fully mobile social service that is available 24 hours a day. Many crises that police respond to include violence in the family and the aftermath of this violence for women and children. Some police forces have developed specialized crisis intervention services (Jaffe et al., 1984) that help officers respond to their calls and make referrals to appropriate community services. Children's mental health centers are one of these services that can respond quickly and view the crisis as an opportunity for an effective intervention. Involving officers or police crisis counselors in case conferences may help center staff to identify important family issues and prioritize the areas for treatment.

The link between a children's mental center and a shelter is also a very important part of the network for battered women and their children, because misunderstandings can sometimes occur between those agencies. Shelters may perceive the centers to be unresponsive to referrals because of long waiting lists and a bias toward highly motivated clients. On the other hand, children's mental health centers may perceive shelter staff as having less clinical training and being too narrowly focused in their advocacy for battered women. These attitudinal barriers can be removed by encouraging staff in both agencies to work together at case conferences and to present to each other's staff meetings. These encounters will facilitate the referrals that need to go in both directions when violence and child adjustment problems are identified by each service. The ultimate form of working together would be for shelter and center staff to develop joint projects such as collaborative group counseling services for children who witness wife assault. In our experience, this kind of project helps develop the various areas of expertise that are required in dealing with these complex family circumstances (Jaffe, Wilson, & Wolfe, 1986).

Children's mental health centers may want to offer their own programs targeted at children of battered women. Unique individual and group counseling programs such as those outlined in Chapter 4 can be developed. These programs signal to the community that this population may have special needs and that the necessary services are available. This knowledge alone may stimulate other community professionals, such as family doctors, clergy, public health nurses, adult mental health center staff, and marriage counselors to identify the needs of their clients' children and make appropriate referrals.

ISSUES FOR CHILD PROTECTION AGENCIES

The field of child abuse has been dominated by the issue of physical abuse of children. More recently, there has been a major shift toward sexual abuse of children, which has been triggered by a dramatic increase in awareness programs and disclosures of sexual victimization. An emerging area of research still in its infancy is emotional abuse and psychological maltreatment (Brassard et al., 1987). Children who witness violence in their family seem to fit all the criteria for emotional abuse in that their normal social, emotional, and cognitive development is being placed at risk as a result of the violence that they are being exposed to in the family.

There is considerable controversy about the role of child protection services with these children. Mandated interventions through legislation, such as reporting responsibilities and required investigations, are vague or nonexistent. For example, out of ten Canadian provinces only two (Newfoundland and Alberta) make specific reference in their child welfare legislation that children who witness violence or severe conflict in their families may be in need of protection (Jaffe, Wilson, Cameron, Zajc, & Wolfe, 1987).

In general, most staff in child protection services already feel overwhelmed with the reports of physical and sexual abuse of children. The high number of disclosures combined with the complexities of investigations, court proceedings, and counseling victims and parents create a great deal of stress for frontline staff. They often do not have the time or energy to consider a whole new dimension of abuse defined by psychological maltreatment and exposure to violence. Shelters may not encourage an active role by child protection agencies because of a concern about revictimizing battered women. Women's fear of losing their children by being declared incompetent parents would be a further trauma to the physical and emotional abuse they have suffered from their husbands. Shelters also worry that general knowledge of a close working relationship between themselves and child protection services may discourage battered women in the community from even seeking safety for fear their children may be taken from them.

We argue that child protection services have a major role in providing assistance for battered women and their children. Although we acknowledge a lack of resources in many jurisdictions to expand this role, this issue becomes a catch-22. That is, the needs are not identified and, therefore, the services cannot be developed through advocacy of government and private funding.

Cummings and Mooney (1988) have suggested several areas of concern that child advocates must address with this population. These include the extent to which children in these families are direct victims of violence in consideration of the significant overlap between witnesses and victims (Levine, 1975); the mother's ability to protect the children from further abuse; the children's social, emotional, and cognitive development living with violence; the impact of victimization on the mother's effectiveness as a parent; and older children's victimization of their siblings as a result of the violence they have witnessed. Cummings and Mooney (1988) have suggested the importance of collaborative efforts of child protection services and shelters through professional development workshops, case conferences, and joint client interviews.

Ultimately, both shelters and child protection services share the goal of ending violence in the family. Although each agency may differ in the focus of its advocacy, joint efforts will provide a higher level of coordinated services for battered women and their children. Recognizing the fact that children who are exposed to violence may be in need of protection also sends a clear message to the community about the life conditions of battered women and their children. It changes wife abuse from being a private family matter between consenting adults to a dangerous situation that may have serious physical and emotional consequences for battered women and their children. In responding to these children, communities may also be made aware of the intergenerational aspects of family violence and the hope that an effective intervention may prevent the next generation of batterers and victims (Jaffe et al., 1987).

CHILDREN IN THE COURT SYSTEM

Battered women and their children also may face a complicated array of police, medical, and social services once the violence is disclosed. Emergency rooms in health care facilities (Klingbeil & Boyd, 1984) and police officers (Jaffe et al., 1984) may be important frontline services in connecting these victims of violence to appropriate community agencies. Shelters, child protection services, and children's mental health centers may offer some valuable counseling programs in certain communities. However, the one system that is often inevitable in the aftermath of violence is the one least prepared for battered women and their children—the justice system. Women and children may find themselves in criminal proceedings if charges of assault are filed and in civil proceedings if custody and financial support become vital issues (Jaffe, Austin, Leschied, & Sas, 1987). Most battered woman report that the justice system is a complicated maze, which may only offer a host of new problems rather than solve the existing ones (Leighton, 1989).

Children of battered women present a special challenge to the justice system. Younger children may be the only witnesses to their mother's victimization and may have to participate in the court proceedings to testify in regard to criminal charges brought against their father. Children may be the central issues in civil proceedings in regard to custody and visitation disputes after separation. Adolescents may become involved in delinquencies that relate directly to the violence they have been exposed to in their family. Consider the following cases that were referred to a court-related clerical assessment service by judges.

> A 7-year-old was the only witness to her father's brutal stabbing of her mother. Her father claims that the death was an accident related to mutual drunkenness and his self-defense after his wife attacked him. The young girl, however, can provide an extremely detailed story to the contrary. She will be challenged in her testimony by a skilled defense lawyer who will question her reliability as a witness. Her emotional state is fragile in that she is trying to deal with the trauma she witnessed, her grief over her mother's death, her ambivalent feelings toward her father, and her sense of rejection from an extended family system that already blames her for her father being denied bail.

> Two young brothers, 10 and 8 years of age, have remained in their mother's custody since the parent's separation one year ago. They have witnessed several years of profound emotional and physical abuse of their mother by their father. They idolize the father who has never abused them directly. He tells them that it is their mother's fault that the family is no longer together and that he wishes to have sole custody of them. The older boy is already beginning to swear at and belittle his mother in a fashion demonstrated by his father. Both boys have become discipline problems for their mother. They tell the judge in his chambers that they wish to live with their father.

> A 15-year-old boy is charged with attempted murder after he tries to shoot his stepfather with a .22 caliber rifle. The prosecutor believes that this offense is serious enough that the boy should be transferred to the adult criminal court so that, if convicted, he can receive a lengthy jail term to protect the community. The boy has witnessed 10 years of assaults by his stepfather on his mother, almost on a weekly basis. The rifle he used is the one that his

stepfather bought several years ago and has pointed at his mother on a regular basis in recent months to threaten her whenever she spoke of separation.

These actual case illustrations offer important reasons why judges and lawyers have had to become more aware of wife abuse and the impact of this violence on women and their children. Judges are forced to deal with complex dilemmas that require a high level of expertise and consultation from court-related clinical services. A decade ago, the resolution of these cases may have been very simple (the charges would have been dropped, the father given custody, and the boy sent to jail, respectively, in the three case illustrations). However, current knowledge of battered women and their children requires many sensitive questions to be asked and a more appropriate court intervention to be offered. The following subsections will examine the three issues raised in the case illustrations: children as witnesses in court, children in custody disputes, and children as young offenders.

Children as Court Witnesses

Children not only witness their mother being assaulted but in many cases they have the ultimate responsibility of being the only ones who can validate the reality of their mother's victimization. In one study of court proceedings on cases of wife assault, which involved over 1,000 victims, one-half of the witnesses who testified were children (Dobash, 1977).

Children are at a disadvantage in testifying in court in a number of ways. Most courts have been very slow to respond to the special needs of children by making the court a friendly and child-centered experience. Courts are an adult world that depends on a high level of verbal skills and an understanding of complex, abstract concepts about an oath, truth, and justice. Children may not be accepted as witnesses because of their age, stage of development, and level of maturity. Even older children may be considered unreliable witnesses with poor memories or as victims of an active fantasy life (Goodman & Rosenberg, 1987).

Children of battered women also face additional personal stressors in testifying in court beyond the normal pressure on all children in this situation. Children who witness violence in their home will feel a sense of divided loyalties toward their parents. They know they have to tell the truth but may feel responsible for the consequences to their father if he receives a stiff court sentence. They may also fear the consequence from their father for themselves or their mother in the event that prosecution leads to a conviction. The entire process before, during, and after the court appearances may stretch into many months and even years of family pressure and anxiety about the process and possible outcomes.

Historically, very few services have been available to children who testify in court. Challenges to children's truthfulness and credibility have turned court into an ordeal that may further victimize these children who have already suffered enough from the consequence of the violence in their family. Often, mental health professionals have been called reluctantly to give forensic evidence in court about children's memory and maturity (Goodman & Rosenberg, 1987).

Some encouraging pilot projects have been reported that have begun to address the special needs of these children (Hurley, Sas, & Wilson, 1988). These projects, often known as court preparation programs, help children to understand the court process from their own knowledge base and perspective as well as to find appropriate coping strategies to deal with their anxiety and confusion. Of special importance to these children is the clarification of their limited role as a witness and how it differs from the responsibilities of the defense lawyer, prosecutor, judge, and jury (in some cases). These interventions are desperately needed because court proceedings represent just one more crisis for many children who are struggling with many other parallel disruptions in their lives.

Children in Custody/Visitation Disputes

Children of battered women are often victimized by prolonged legal disputes about which parent should have custody after separation or what kind of visitation schedule is reasonable. The legal battle is never one moment in time but rather a drawn-out affair over many years with a history of threats and conflicts, which many of the children discover continues long after the separation and long after any court decisions.

Even before the separation, many battered women are threatened with the fact that their husbands will want custody of the children if the women decide to leave. Often this threat will be a central issue in keeping a women prisoner in her own home for fear of this and other consequences (NiCarthy, 1982). Women who feel most vulnerable in these circumstances are ones who believe that, because their husbands have never *directly* abused the children, the husbands would have a good opportunity to be awarded custody. Many of these women will describe their husbands as better suited for the court battle because of the husbands' ability to "charm and con selected important people for short-term interactions" required by this process (Walker & Edwall, 1987). Men's rights groups created a backlash to this view by suggesting that their rights as fathers have been ignored (e.g., Roman & Haddad, 1978).

Several authors have suggested that battered women's anxiety about court is well founded, in light of a strong bias in many judges' minds about a father's rights to his children (Chesler, 1986; Walker, 1989). Chesler (1986), in her recent book titled *Mothers on Trial: The Battle for Children and Custody*, indicated that nearly two-thirds of the women she interviewed felt "legally or judicially battered" by the process they had to endure in seeking custody of their children. She described several case studies involving women who had been the primary caretakers of children ultimately being prevented from any reasonable contact with them. From her reports, the fathers on the other side of these disputes were often uninvolved parents and abusive men. This abuse was not considered a relevant factor in the cases reported.

Judges and family lawyers have been increasingly challenged to examine their knowledge and attitudes in the area of family violence. The special issues that face battered women and their children in custody disputes are a major impetus for the development of new policies and services. Three important examples are the emerging role of custody evaluations (assessments), mediation, and supervised visitation centers.

More family lawyers and judges are turning to mental health professionals to assist in the resolution of custody disputes through the preparation of clinical assessments of each parent and the children (Jaffe, Austin, Leschied, & Sas, 1987). These assessments help to focus the court on the "best interest of the children" following parental separation. However, many professionals preparing these evaluations may also lack information and awareness about family violence. It is surprising that a recent book about custody assessments left out the topic of violence except to warn professionals to be cautious about exaggerated reports of violence by women (Parry, Broder, Schmitt, Saunders, & Hood, 1986).

Walker and Edwall (1987) offer many helpful suggestions in dealing with battered women and their children in the legal field. They outline several important assessment steps, such as separate interviews for each parent that include a detailed history of violence from the perspective of the adults and children involved. The children's emotional and behavioral adjustment related to these experiences is considered to be a major dimension of the assessment.

Mediation services have become a popular alternative to the adversarial process involved in custody litigation (e.g., Coogler, 1978; Irving, 1980).

Mediation involves joint interviews between the parents and an impartial third party to help them work out a mutually agreeable resolution of custody and visitation conflicts. Although this intervention assists many couples, special caution has to be offered for this approach when addressing the concerns of battered women and their children. Mediation assumes some balance of power between parents, which is not possible when a mother lives in fear of the children's father (Lerman, 1984).

Because the mediational process encourages cooperation and compromise, a battered women may be put in the position of appearing rigid and uncooperative because of her fear for the safety of herself and her children (Boyd, 1987; Walker & Edwall, 1987). Moreover, courts often support the parent who can best promote child access to the other parent. If a battered women appears to be a "less friendly" parent (e.g., fearful, apprehensive, cautious), she may lose custody of the children to her husband. A secondary danger is the reality that children's needs may become overlooked in the mediator's attempt to find a compromise between two adults. Alternate-weekend access for a father may be a "reasonable deal," but such an arrangement may not recognize the trauma the children have experienced by witnessing the abuse of their mother (Walker & Edwall, 1987). The ultimate issue of mediation rests with the qualification, training, and sensitivity of mediators to deal with this special population (Ministry of the Attorney General, 1989).

Supervised visitation or access centers are a recent innovation that offers a neutral, safe location for children to see their noncustodial parent without exposure to more conflict and potentially violent behavior (Lubell & Dibbs, 1987). For children of battered women, this service may fulfill an essential need because many abusive husbands will use visitation as an opportunity to harass and continue to threaten their partners (Sonkin, Martin, & Walker, 1985). A recent Toronto study of 235 battered women indicated that 25% of women with children reported that their husband continued to make threats against their lives during visitation and 5% reported threats of kidnapping (Leighton, 1989). Staff at access centers can facilitate visitation for many children who continue to love their father but who remain fearful of his anger and violence directed at their mother. Skilled interventions can assist children in expressing feelings that are often aroused before and after such contact. Except in extreme situations where death threats and kidnapping represent real possibilities, some access even on a limited basis is important. In our experience, children of battered women who are totally cut off from any contact with their father may grow to idealize him and seek out contact as soon as the first conflicts of adolescence emerge.

Courts may become more responsive to the needs of battered women and their children as more information and specialized resources are offered to them. When the courts feel that they have enough input from informed professionals working with these children and when resources are made available to deal with very practical dilemmas, new attitudes may be fostered. The following report of a recent Ontario court judgment may be a sign of a more enlightened period.

> In divorce petition, major corollary issues were custody, division of property, and support. Parties had separated in 1985 after more than 17 years of marriage. They had a daughter aged 14 and a son aged 12. Husband, 39, was a chartered accountant and wife, also 39, was a teacher. Both worked full-time. Wife had primary responsibility for care of children during marriage. Following separation, she had sought psychological counseling. Psychologist testified that she had suffered from effects of verbal, emotional, physical, and sexual abuse by husband, but that her condition had improved with therapy. Husband had commenced cohabitation with another woman in 1988. Children had expressed desire to live with husband, with wife to have liberal access. Hold: Wife entitled to custody of children with liberal access to husband. Court accepted wife's evidence that husband had abused her, as well as expert evidence that abuser who went without therapy would continue abuse in another relationship, that children who witnessed abuse could become abused even though abuse was not intentionally directed at them, and that abused male children often become abusers and abused female children might become compliant to abuse. In such circumstances, and in view of certain manipulative behavior of husband with respect to children, it was in best interests of children that wife have custody. Children were too young to give paramountcy to their stated desire to live with husband. (*Young v. Young*, 1988)

Adolescents in the Juvenile Justice System

Children who live in violent families often proceed through different aspects of the court system as they enter adolescence. Younger children who were involved in child protection hearings or who participated as pawns in custody disputes may emerge into the juvenile justice system as young offenders. Violent families encourage the development of several serious adjustment problems, which often lead to police and court intervention focused on delinquent behavior. Girls may come to the attention of the court because of unmanageable behavior, including running away and involvement in juvenile prostitution. Boys may begin to engage in the violent behavior they have witnessed in their home and face assault charges in the court (Rutter & Giller, 1983).

Most authorities in the field of juvenile delinquency look to conditions in the home environment as a major contributor to antisocial behavior (Rutter & Giller, 1983). This behavior is often modeled very clearly at home. When children learn that violence can resolve conflict in the home, and the police and courts do not respond to their father's behavior, they are often surprised to learn that the juvenile system may see this behavior in a different light. An understanding of this behavior always requires a close examination of the parents' relationship with each other and with their children. All too often minor offenses may be related to violence and disorganization in the home that allow for minimal supervision of adolescents (Rutter & Giller, 1983). More extreme suicidal and assaultive behavior can often be traced to a number of factors in the family, including the children's exposure to violence (e.g., Pfeffer, Plutchik, & Mizruchi, 1983). Lewis et al. (1979) found that witnessing violence was an even more distinguishing feature of assaultive boy's childhood experiences in comparison with direct physical abuse. In this research, 97 boys who were residents in a juvenile correctional facility were assessed for level of violence based on their current behavior and past offenses. Four times as many boys in the most violent group had witnessed violence in their home's in comparison with the least violent group (79% versus 20%). The impact of being abused by either parent or another person doubled the probability of being in the most violent group (Lewis et al., 1979).

These findings suggest the importance of the juvenile justice system in developing appropriate early intervention or prevention services, assessment services, and correctional programs that address the issue of family violence. Police officers often have unique opportunities for early intervention with these families when they respond to domestic disputes, which represent a significant portion of their work. Officers who are aware of the impact of violence on child witnesses may be able to provide clear statements on the inappropriateness of this behavior and heighten a batterer's insight as to how his behavior affects his wife directly and the children indirectly. Well-trained police forces can maximize the utilization of the criminal justice system and referrals to appropriate social service/mental health agencies to deal with these issues. Police forces can gain an additional benefit by utilizing specialized staff within their departments to offer consultation to officers on crisis management and facilitate referrals between law enforcement and social service professionals (Jaffe et al., 1984).

Juvenile court judges are often faced with difficult dilemmas in balancing a young person's rights and his or her special needs. Children and adolescents of battered women present one of these dilemmas when the court can see a clear link between violence in the home and a young person's violence in the community. Unfortunately, in many cases the young person's behavior is a well-established pattern of responding to stress or conflict. This behavior may be well reinforced by a sense of power and control in an adolescent, which helps him or her cope with an otherwise dismal and frustrating life experience. Consequently, simple court intervention is unlikely to be successful. A first step is for the court to obtain a comprehensive social history or a court-related clinical assessment. These assessments may be crucial in helping the judge fully appreciate the role of violence in the family and may suggest a number of intervention strategies (Jaffe, Wolfe, Wilson, & Zak, 1985). In our experience, almost half of young offenders who were referred by juvenile court judges for clinical assessments had witnessed violence in the family when the presenting charges were related to assaults, based on 80 cases (London Family Court Clinic, 1987-1988).

Delinquent youth are often served by probation officers who monitor their behavior in the community or by correctional staff who observe their behavior in detention and custody placements. For a large proportion of these delinquents, dealing with the violence they have witnessed or experienced directly will be a major rehabilitation and management goal. Residential and nonresidential programs that can deal directly with behavior and attitude toward violence are an essential component of an effective correctional intervention. Many of the same programs that have been developed to help battered women deal with their victimization and batterers deal with their violence can be tailored for an adolescent population in the correctional system. Without these innovations, this system will simply process offenders and create more disruptions for youth who will repeat violent offenses (Rutter & Giller, 1983).

A CHALLENGE FOR SCHOOL SYSTEMS

It would be a challenge to find any book written on the topic of family violence that does not end with an appeal to school systems for prevention programs (e.g., Davidson, 1978; Gelles & Straus, 1988; MacLeod, 1989). The appeal is usually expressed as a recognition that underlying societal attitudes condone violence and that only a major commitment by school systems to address this problem can lead to any meaningful changes.

Usually these wishes are vague and lack specific suggestions or concrete examples of what schools have actually done. This book goes beyond these wishes to offer three specific areas that offer a reality base for this issue. These areas relate to teacher training, curriculum development, and student involvement in addressing family violence.

Teachers often feel that societal expectations of schools are excessive. Most teachers feel that reading, writing, and arithmetic in crowded classrooms are enough of a challenge without addressing major social problems like alcohol and drug abuse, AIDS, teen pregnancy, suicide, and violence in the family. The reality, however, is that teachers must address these issues directly or indirectly on a daily basis whether or not they want to. For example, the current estimates of wife battering suggest that anywhere from three to five children in each classroom may be witnessing violence in their homes (Kincaid, 1982). Interventions aimed at increasing teacher awareness must recognize this prevailing situation and offer additional resources and consultation to match increasing expectations.

In the 1990s it will be nearly impossible to be an effective teacher without knowing about family violence and its direct and indirect impact on students. The goals of any workshops or professional development sessions with teachers should include offering the following information:

Wife abuse is a major social and criminal problem in our society.
Children are affected directly and indirectly by the violence they witness.
This impact may affect children's academic, social, and emotional adjustment in a way that requires special interventions by the school system.
Teachers are important role models in regard to conflict resolution and the diverse roles of men and women.
Resources are available in the school system to help students who disclose violent behavior in their families.
Specialized resources are available in the community to assist battered women, assaultive men, and child witnesses to violence.

In our experience of presenting workshops on this topic to educators in our province, we have received a very positive response. We have been encouraged by the leadership role the government has taken by offering each school board incentive funding for these programs and recommending broad involvement of school trustees, senior administrators, principals, counselors, and classroom teachers. In the public education system in our local community, which includes 42,000 students in 67 elementary and 15 secondary schools, full-day workshops were offered to all principals and selected staff. As part of these workshops, small discussion groups generated the following list of recommendations for the system action plan:

heighten the awareness of all teaching staff of the prevalence and implications of domestic violence in our community and on our students;
develop a plan and/or procedure in all schools to deal with student disclosure of family violence, much like the child abuse policy;
make awareness presentations on domestic violence to home and school associations;
prepare a package of material to be sent to every student's home including key phone numbers to be placed on refrigerators;
set up display posters with resource material in guidance or resource areas with tear-off telephone numbers;
broaden the community's coordinating committee on family violence to include education representations;
keep the Crisis Contact Book up to date and make it more available in schools;
teach students in primary grades ways of resolving peer disputes and how to express anger appropriately;
introduce the topic of domestic violence in school curriculum where appropriate;
make greater use of the resources within and without the educational system, such as videos, films, health curriculum information, and community resource personnel, to help with discussions on topics that are extremely sensitive and/or disturbing, such as family violence, child abuse, and date abuse;
develop special kits for young women to highlight issues around domestic violence and/or date violence;
develop an in-school suspension program to include a three-day training program on "controlling your anger";
require more access to psychological services, social work, and/or child-care services by schools;
develop a model interview and/or questions for teachers to use to explore issues of family violence and/or abuse;
address safety issues related to family violence with students in conjunction with street proofing, block parent, emergency numbers, and so on;
stress that schools, principals, vice principals, and teachers need to act as role models in dealing with violence—there is a need to accentuate the message that violent behavior in any circumstances will not be tolerated;
address the major issues around "ownership" of the problems surrounding family violence—teachers need to realize that they cannot take on this huge responsibility alone; it is important to make the distinction among the various issues (e.g., identification, support, referral, preventions, and interventions); teachers can "own" a small part of one or all of these issues, but ultimately a cooperative community effort is required to tackle these issues;

ensure that referrals to community resources are reasoned responses that provide confidence and trust in working relations between the board of education and the community agencies.

These suggestions are not offered as the answer to a complicated problem. Rather, this list was generated to indicate the energy and commitment to an issue like wife assault that is possible among better-informed educators.

A second step in the schools' response to this issue has to be curriculum development. As teachers become aware of a new problem area, they may seek out or want to develop curriculum materials that can assist them in teaching students at different grade levels. Concrete resources and reading lists have to form a major part of reinforcing initial efforts in this endeavor. Although some resistance is expected from parents as to the appropriateness of school involvement in this issue, evidence exists to suggest the reverse. Parents can be active partners and advocates in the development of new curriculum materials (Knicely, 1988).

The most advanced curriculum in this field is available from the Minnesota Coalition of Battered Women (Stavrou-Petersen & Gamache, 1988), which has developed an extensive package of material to challenge existing sex role stereotypes and the view that violence relates to power and control. Alternative conflict-resolution strategies are highlighted. An exciting part of this curriculum is the direct approach to adolescents who face these issues directly in dating and in the development of the first intimate relationships outside their families. Given the high incidence of violence against teenagers in such relationships (Mercer, 1987), this material is very timely. An initial evaluation of this program is very encouraging in regard to high school students gaining knowledge about family violence based on a comparison of several hundred students who received this program from specially trained teachers and a control group, matched for grade level and school district (Jones, 1987).

Adolescents can be excellent partners in changing prevailing attitudes and behavior regarding family violence. The success of programs addressing changes in smoking behavior, diet and exercise, and drunk driving augers well for family violence prevention. Recent workshops that we have organized for teenagers on this topic have found a very striking openness on the part of this population. The majority of adolescents welcomed the discussion, felt their schools should be more active in dealing with the problem, and offered many creative ideas (Ontario Psychological Foundation, 1989). Some of the suggestions students offered are available in a detailed report (Jaffe & Reitzel, in press). Several examples of student comments are these:

Preparation-for-parents courses are necessary so that people know what to expect when they become parents.

One of the basic problems is that no one knows where to go or what to do. There should be family studies courses in public school on relationships or communication courses just on communication at every level, and [they should be made] compulsory.

How do you tell someone close to you that they are tending to be violent? The fact that there isn't the communication in the home, there isn't the communication between partners, is why a lot of this happens, because they're not willing to sit down and talk and get their feelings out that way. They resort to things such as abuse. So that's one of the basic problems behind what we're dealing with today.

[Our] discussion group decided that there should be mandatory counseling in schools. . . . Some sort of mandatory counseling might be a good idea because then if you were seen going to counseling, your friends might not necessarily think, "Oh, this person has a problem," because it's mandatory to go there.

[Our] group discussed the possibilities of volunteer groups in schools, because kids can talk to kids their own age much easier. If teenagers volunteered and were trained to deal with teenage crisis situations, then perhaps teenagers would feel more at ease talking to other teenagers about their problems.

We also suggested making a video. . . . If we made a video about a date rape, and showed it in classes, people would be able to see that and say, "Yeah, I think that happened to a friend of mine," and they'd be a lot more willing to tell people about it because they know it's happening to other people.

Current social values should be challenged in schools by students of any age, and these social values include men's and women's roles in society, what they are, what they should be, what we feel they should be.

The second [idea] was sexual stereotypes. Something that's really been changing in the past few years is how society has used men and how society has used women, but it's something that still has to change more. We still have that sexual stereotype of the male being strong, the woman being weak, and so on. And the definite problem behind this whole area of concern is that women don't see themselves as—I don't know if it's equal to men, if that's the right word—but they're just not as assertive and they're not as confident in dealing with men, and men seem to be overconfident in dealing with women.

> We also talked about the isolation and the alienation of someone who has been abused, and that's a real problem because it stops them from going and looking for help because they feel alone and rejected, and they're afraid to tell someone because of the way they'll be treated.
>
> We also mentioned the denial. . . . I think that's also part of society accepting it as something that does happen; so we have to change basically the values of society, as in the stereotyping, and what is accepted and what you can say, what you can tell people, so people feel more at ease telling someone this and going for help.
>
> Examine how you can help teens wanting to help other teens trying to operate in a group atmosphere instead of being all alone.
>
> We found that kids related to other kids. Teenagers relate to friends, a girlfriend, a person they sit beside in class. What should these people do? If you hear that someone is having a problem, what can you do about it?
>
> We found that if we put posters up in the school, advertising special groups where you could come and have current events talked about, the people could all of a sudden discover that they have similar crises in the family.

We have been very stimulated by these adolescent's willingness to openly discuss violence in relationships and offer meaningful suggestions for a violence-free society. Their enthusiasm is contagious not only for their peers and teachers but also for professionals like ourselves who struggle with the stress of reaching out to victims of violence. We sense that the school system presents a new frontier in developing well-conceptualized primary prevention programs. There is no quick fix to end violence and its impact on battered women and their children. However, we can see a light at the other end of a long tunnel.

SUMMARY

This final chapter has considered the implications of the growing knowledge about child witnesses to wife assault for the delivery of children's services. Awareness of the special needs of this population should help service providers in a number of settings, such as children's mental health centers, child protection agencies, and school systems, to ask two fundamental questions: First, are our staff members open and sensitive to the possibility that some children live with violence and may suffer from a broad range of adjustment problems? Second, what intervention strategies can our staff develop to respond to the needs of these children in collaboration with other community agencies? We hope more professionals in children's services ask these questions and develop increasingly effective responses.

REFERENCES

Achenbach, T. M., & Edelbrock, C. S. (1983). *Manual for the child behavior checklist and revised child behavior profile*. Burlington, VT: University Associates in Psychiatry.

Alessi, J. J., & Hearn, K. (1984). Group treatment of children in shelters for battered women. In A. R. Roberts (Ed.), *Battered women and their families* (pp. 49–61). New York: Springer.

Alexander, J. F., & Parsons, B. V. (1982). *Functional family therapy*. Monterey, CA: Brooks/Cole.

American Psychiatric Association. (1987). *Diagnostic and statistical manual of mental disorders* (3rd. ed., rev.). Washington, DC: Author.

Armstrong, D. T. (1986). Shelter based parenting services: A skill building process. *Children Today*, pp. 16–20.

Ayalon, O., & Van Tassel, E. (1987). Living in dangerous environments. In M. R. Brassard, R. Germain, & S. N. Hart (Eds.), *Psychological maltreatment of children and youth* (pp. 171–182). New York: Pergamon.

Bandura, A. (1973). *Aggression: A social learning analysis*. Englewood Cliffs, NJ: Prentice-Hall.

Bard, M. (1970). Role of law enforcement in the helping system. In J. Monahan (Ed.), *Community mental health and the criminal justice system* (pp. 99–109). Elmsford, NJ: Pergamon.

Bowker, L. H., Arbittel, M., & McFerron, J. R. (1988). On the relationship between wife beating and child abuse. In K. Yllö & M. Bograd (Eds.), *Feminist perspectives on wife abuse* (pp. 158–174). Beverly Hills, CA: Sage.

Bowlby, J. (1973). *Attachment and loss: Separation* (Vol. 2). New York: Basic Books.

Boyd, S. B. (1987). *Child custody, ideologies and female employment*. Paper presented at the workshop, "Working Women and Custody issues," National Association on Women and the Law, biennial conference, Winnipeg, Manitoba.

Brassard, M. R., Germain, R., & Hart, S. N. (1987). The challenge: To better understand and combat psychological maltreatment of children and youth. In M. R. Brassard, R. Germain, & S. N. Hart (Eds.), *Psychological maltreatment of children and youth* (pp. 3–24). New York: Pergamon.

Bretherton, I., Fritz, J., Zahn-Waxler, C., & Ridgeway, D. (1986). Learning to talk about emotions: A functionalist perspective. *Child Development, 57*, 529–548.

Brody, G. H., & Forehand, R. (1986). Maternal perceptions of child maladjustment as a function of the combined influence of child behavior and maternal depression. *Journal of Consulting and Clinical Psychology, 54*(3), 237–240.

Browne, A. (1987). *When battered women kill*. New York: Free Press.

Carlson, B. E. (1984). Children's observations of interparental violence. In A. R. Roberts (Ed.), *Battered women and their families* (pp. 147–167). New York: Springer.

Cassady, L., Allen, B., Lyon, E., & McGeehan, D. (1987, July). *The Child-focused intervention program: Treatment and program evaluation for children in a battered women's shelter*. Paper presented at the Third National Family Violence Researchers' Conference, Durham, NH.

Chesler, P. (1986). *Mothers on trial: The battle for children & custody*. Seattle: Seal Press.

Christensen, A., Phillips, S., Glasgow, R. E., & Johnson, S. M. (1983). Parental characteristics and interactional dysfunction in families with child behavior problems: A preliminary investigation. *Journal of Abnormal Child Psychology, 11*, 153–166.

Coogler, O. J. (1978). *Structured mediation in divorce settlement*. Lexington, MA: Lexington.

Covell, D., & Abramovitch, R. (1987). Understanding emotion in the family: Children's and parents' attributions of happiness, sadness, and anger. *Child Development, 58*, 985–991.

Covell, K., & Abramovitch, R. (in press). Children's understanding of maternal anger: Age and source of anger differences. *Merrill-Palmer Quarterly*.

Crockenberg, S. (1985). Toddlers' reactions to maternal anger. *Merrill-Palmer Quarterly, 31*, 361–373.

Cummings, E. M. (1987). Coping with background anger in early childhood. *Child Development, 58*, 976–984.

Cummings, E. M., Iannotti, R. J., & Zahn-Waxler, C. (1985). Influence of conflict between adults on the emotions and aggression of young children. *Developmental Psychology, 21* 495–507.

Cummings, E. M., Zahn-Waxler, C., & Radke-Yarrow, M. (1981). Young children's responses to expressions of anger and affection by others in the family. *Child Development, 52*, 1274–1282.

Cummings, N., & Mooney, A. (1988). Child protective workers and battered women's advocates: A strategy for family violence intervention. *Response, 11*, 4–9.

Davidson, T. (1978). *Conjugal crime: Understanding and changing the wife beating pattern*. New York: Hawthorn.

deLange, C. (1986, March/April). The Family Place children's therapeutic program. *Children's Today*, pp. 12–15.

Dobash, R. E. (1977). *The relationship between violence directed at women and violence directed at children within the family setting*. London: House of Commons, Select Committee on Violence in the Family.

Dobash, R. E., & Dobash, R. (1979). *Violence against wives: A case against the patriarchy*. New York: Free Press.

Dumas, J., & Wahler, R. G. (1985). Indiscriminate mothering as a contextual factor in aggressive-oppositional child behavior: "Damned if you do, damned if you don't." *Journal of Abnormal Child Psychology, 13*, 1–17.

Dutton, D. G. (1988). *The domestic assault of women: Psychological and criminal justice perspectives*. Toronto: Allyn & Bacon.

Eckenrode, J., & Gore, S. (1981). Stressful events and social supports: The significance of context. In B. Gottlieb (Ed.), *Social networks and social support* (pp. 43–68). Beverly Hills, CA: Sage.

Emery, R. E. (1982). Interparental conflict and the children of discord and divorce. *Psychological Bulletin, 92*, 310–330.

Emery, R. E. (1989). Family violence. *American Psychologist, 44*, 321–328.

Emery, R., Kraft, S. P., Joyce, S., & Shaw, D. (1984, August). *Children of abused women: Adjustment at four months following shelter residence*. Paper presented at the annual meeting of the American Psychological Association, Toronto.

Emery, R. E., & O'Leary, K. D. (1982). Children's perceptions of marital discord and behavior problems of boys and girls. *Journal of Abnormal Psychology, 10*, 11–42.

Erickson, E. (1963). *Childhood and society*. New York: Norton.

Factor, D., & Wolfe, D. A. (in press). Parental psychopathology. In R. T. Ammerman & M. Hersen (Eds.), *Children at risk: An evaluation of factors contributing to child abuse and neglect*. New York: Plenum.

Fagan, J. (1983). Stress and coping in early development. In N. Garmezy & M. Rutter (Eds.), *Stress, coping, and development in children* (pp. 191–216). New York: McGraw-Hill.

Fagan, J., & Wexler, S. (1987). Family origins of violent delinquents. *Criminology, 25*, 643–669.

Fantuzzo, J. W., & Lindquist, C. U. (1989). The effects of observing conjugal violence on children: A review and analysis of research methodology. *Journal of Family Violence, 4*, 77–94.

Feinman, S. (1982). Social referencing in infancy. *Merrill-Palmer Quarterly, 28*, 445–470.

Finkelhor, D., Gelles, R. J., Hotaling, G. T., & Straus, M. A. (Eds.). (1983). *The dark side of families: Current family violence research*. Beverly Hills, CA: Sage.

Flannery, R. B., Jr. (1987). From victim to survivor: A stress management approach in the treatment of learned helplessness (pp. 217–232). In B. A. Van der Kolk (Ed.), *Psychological trauma*. Washington, DC: American Psychiatric Press.

Friedrich-Cofer, L. T., & Huston, A. C. (1986). Television violence and aggression: The debate continues. *Psychological Bulletin, 100*(3), 364–371.

Garbarino, J., & Gillian, G. (1980). *Understanding abusive families*. Toronto: Lexington.

Garmezy, N. (1983). Stressors of childhood. In N. Garmezy & M. Rutter (Eds.), *Stress, coping, and development in children* (pp. 43–84). New York: McGraw-Hill.

Gayford, J. J. (1975). Wife battering: A preliminary survey of 100 cases. *British Medical Journal, 1*, 194–197.

Gelles, R. J. (1975). Violence and pregnancy: A note on the extent of the problem and needed services. *Family Coordinator, 24*, 81–86.

Gelles, R. J. (1987). *The violent home* (rev. ed.). Newbury Park, CA: Sage.

Gelles, R. J., & Straus, M. A. (1988). *Intimate violence*. New York: Simon & Schuster.

Gentry, C. E., & Eaddy, V. B. (1982). Treatment of children in spouse abusive families. *Victimology: An International Journal, 5*, 240–250.

Gessell, A. (1943). *Infant and child in the culture of today: The guidance of development in home and nursery school*. New York: Harper.

Girardin, L. (1988). *Effects of viewing high and low violence on children on a school versus shelter population*. Unpublished bachelor's thesis, University of Western Ontario, London, Ontario.

Gnepp, J. (1983). Children's social sensitivity: Inferring emotions from conflicting cues. *Developmental Psychology, 19*, 805–814.

Goodman, G. S., & Rosenberg, M. S. (1987). The child witness to family violence: Clinical and legal considerations. In D. Sonkin (Ed.), *Domestic violence on trial* (pp. 97–126). New York: Springer.

Greaves, L., Heapy, N., & Wylie, A. (1988). Reassessing the profile and needs of battered women. *Canadian Journal of Community Mental Health, 7*, 39–51.

Grossier, D. (1986). *Child witnesses to interparental violence: Social problem solving skills and behavioral adjustment*. Unpublished master's thesis, University of Denver, Denver, CO.

Grusznski, R. J., Brink, J. C., & Edleson, J. L. (1988). Support and education groups for children of battered women. *Child Welfare, LXVII* (5), 431–444.

Hart, S. N., & Brassard, M. R. (1987). A major threat to children's mental health: Psychological maltreatment. *American Psychologist, 42*, 160–165.

Harter, S. (1982). A cognitive-developmental approach to children's understanding of affect and trait labels. In F. C. Serafica (Ed.), *Social-cognitive development in context* (pp. 27–61). New York: Guilford.

Hartup, W. W. (1989). Social relationships and their developmental significance. *American Psychologist, 44*, 120–126.

Hazzard, A., Christensen, A., & Margolin, G. (1983). Children's perceptions of parental behaviors. *Journal of Abnormal Child Psychology, 11*, 49–60.

Heath, C., Kruttschnitt, C., & Ward, D. (1986). Television and violent criminal behavior: Beyond the Bobo doll. *Violence and Victims, 1*, 177–190.

Henggeler, S. W. (1989). *Delinquency in adolescence*. Newbury Park, CA: Sage.

Hess, R. D., & Camara, K. A. (1979). Post-divorce family relationships as mediating factors in the consequences of divorce for children. *Journal of Social Issues, 35*, 79–96.

Hetherington, E. M. (1979). Divorce, a child's perspective. *American Psychologist, 34*, 851–858.

Hetherington, E. M., Cox, M., & Cox, R. (1979). Family interaction and the social, emotional, and cognitive development of children following divorce. In V. Vaughn & J. Brazelton (Eds.), *The family: Setting priorities* (pp. 89–128). New York: Science and Medicine.

Hilberman, E., & Munson, K. (1978). Sixty battered women. *Victimology, 2*, 460–470.

Hotaling, G. T., & Sugarman, D. B. (1986). An analysis of risk markers in husband and wife violence: The current state of knowledge. *Violence and Victims, 1*(2), 101–124.

Hughes, H. M. (1982). Brief interventions with children in a battered women's shelter: A model preventive program. *Family Relations, 31*, 495–502.

Hughes, H. M. (1986). Research with children in shelters: Implications for clinical services. *Children Today*, pp. 21–25.

Hughes, H. M. (1988). Psychological & behavioral correlates of family violence in child witnesses & victims. *American Journal of Orthopsychiatry, 18*, 77–90.

Hughes, H. M., & Hampton, K. L. (1984, August). *Relationships between the effective functioning of physically abused and nonabused children and their mothers in shelters for battered women.* Paper presented at the annual meeting of the American Psychological Association, Toronto.

Hughes, H. M., Parkinson, D., & Vargo, M. (1987, August). *Witnessing spouse abuse and experiencing physical abuse: A "double whammy"?* Paper presented at the annual meeting of the American Psychological Association, New York.

Hurley, P., Sas, L., & Wilson, S. (1988). Empowering children for abuse litigations. *Preventing Sexual Abuse, 1*, 8–12.

Irving, H. H. (1980). *Divorce mediation: The rational alternative*. Toronto: Personal Library.

Jaffe, P., Austin, G., Leschied, A., & Sas, L. (1981). Critical issues in the development of custody and access dispute resolution services. *Canadian Journal of Behavioural Science, 19* (4), 405–417.

Jaffe, P., & Burris, C. A. (1984). *An integrated response to wife assault: A community model* (Working Paper No. 1984–27). Ottawa: Solicitor General of Canada.

Jaffe, P., Finlay, J., & Wolfe, D. (1984). Evaluating the impact of a specialized civilian family crisis unit within a police force on the resolution of family conflicts. *Journal of Preventive Psychiatry, 2*, 63–73.

Jaffe, P., & Reitzel, D. (in press). *Adolescents' views on how to reduce family violence: An analysis of responses to a community workshop*. In R. Roesch, D. G. Dutton, and V. S. Sacco, *Family Violence: Perspectives on treatment, research and policy.* Burnaby: Simon Fraser University.

Jaffe, P., & Thompson, J. (1984). Crisis intervention and the London family consultant model. *R.C.M.P. Gazette, 46*, 12–17.

Jaffe, P., Wilson, S., Cameron, S., Zajc, R., & Wolfe, D. (1987). Are children who witness wife battering in need of protection? *Journal of the Ontario Association of Children's Aid Societies, 31*, 3–7.

Jaffe, P., Wilson, S., & Wolfe, D. (1986). Promoting changes in attitudes and understanding of conflict resolution among child witnesses of family violence. *Canadian Journal of Behavioral Science, 18*, 4.

Jaffe, P., Wilson, S. K., & Wolfe, D. (1989). Specific assessment and intervention strategies for children exposed to wife battering: Preliminary empirical investigation. *Canadian Journal of Community Mental Health, 7*, 157–163.

Jaffe, P., Wolfe, D., Telford, A., & Austin, G. (1986). The impact of police charges in incidents of wife abuse. *Journal of Family Violence, 1*(1), 37–49.

Jaffe, P., Wolfe, D., Wilson, S., & Slusczarzck, M. (1985). Similarities in behavior and social maladjustment among child victims and witnesses to family violence. *American Journal of Orthopsychiatry, 56*, 142–146.

Jaffe, P., Wolfe, D., Wilson, S., & Zak, L. (1985). Critical issues in the assessment of children's adjustment to witnessing family violence. *Canada's Mental Health, 33*(4), 15–19.

Jaffe, P., Wolfe, D. A., Wilson, S., & Zak, L. (1986). Emotional and physical health problems of battered women. *Canadian Journal of Psychiatry, 31*, 625–629.

Jones, L. E. (1987). *Minnesota coalition for battered women school curriculum project evaluation report*. Unpublished manuscript, University of Minnesota, School of Social Work, Minneapolis.

Jouriles, E. N., Murphy, C. M., & O'Leary, K. D. (1989). Interspousal aggression, marital discord, and child problems. *Journal of Consulting and Clinical Psychology, 57*, 453–455.

Kalmuss, D. (1984). The intergenerational transmission of marital aggression. *Journal of Marriage and the Family, 46*, 11–19.

Kaufman, J., & Zigler, E. (1987). Do abused children become abusive parents? *American Journal of Orthopsychiatry, 57*, 186–192.

Kazdin, A. E. (1987). *Conduct disorders in childhood and adolescence*. Newbury Park, CA: Sage.

Kelly, J. B., & Wallerstein, J. S. (1976). The effects of parental divorce: Experiences of the child in early latency. *American Journal of Orthopsychiatry, 46*, 20–23.

Kendall, P. C., & Braswell, L. (1985). *Cognitive-behavioral therapy for impulsive children*. New York: Guilford.

Kincaid, P. J. (1982). *The omitted reality: Husband-wife violence in Ontario and policy implications for education*. Concord, Ontario: Belsten.

Klingbeil, K. S., & Boyd, V. D. (1984). Emergency room intervention: Detection, assessment, and treatment. In A. R. Roberts (Ed.), *Battered women and their families* (pp. 5–32). New York: Springer.

Knicely, B. (1988). *An evaluation of the personal safety curriculum*. Unpublished Manuscript, Lincoln County Board of Education, St. Catherines, Ontario.

Kraft, S. P., Sullivan–Hanson, J., Christopoulos, C., Cohn, D. A., & Emery, R. E. (1984, August). *Spouse abuse: Its impact on children's psychological adjustment*. Paper presented at the annual meeting of the American Psychological Association, Toronto.

Krugman, S. (1987). Trauma in the family: Perspectives on the intergenerational transmission of violence. In B. A. Van der Kolk (Ed.), *Psychological trauma* (pp. 127–151). Washington, DC: American Psychiatric Press.

Kurdek, L. A. (1981). An integrative perspective on children's divorce adjustment. *American Psychologist, 36*, 856–866.

Langley, R., & Levy, R. C. (1977). *Wife beating: The silent crisis*. New York: E. P. Dutton.

Layzer, J. I., Goodson, B. D., & deLange, C. (1985). Children in shelters. *Response, 9*(2), 2–5.

Leighton, B. (1989). *Spousal abuse in metropolitan Toronto: Research report on the response of the criminal justice system* (Report No. 1989–02). Ottawa: Solicitor General of Canada.

Lerman, L. G. (1984). Mediation of wife abuse cases: The adverse impact of informal dispute resolution on women. *Harvard Women's Law Journal, 1*, 57–113.

Levine, M. B. (1975). Interparental violence and its effect on the children: A study of 50 families in general practice. *Medicine, Science, and the Law, 15*(3), 172–176.

Levy, B. (1984). *Skills for violence-free relationships*. Santa Monica: Southern California Coalition for Battered Women.

Lewis, D. O., Shanok, S. S., Pincus, J. H., & Glaser, G. H. (1979). Violent juvenile delinquents: Psychiatric, neurological, psychological, and abuse factors. *Journal of the American Academy of Child Psychiatry, 18*, 307–319.

London Family Court Clinic. (1987–1988). *Annual report*. London, Ontario: Author.

Lowrey, S. A., & DeFleur, M. L. (1988). *Milestones in mass communication research: Media effects* (2nd ed.). New York: Longman.

Lubell, J. E., & Dibbs, L. (1987). The Merrimount Supervised Access program: Meeting the needs of children in the post separation crisis. *Canadian Children: Journal of the Canadian Association for Young Children, 12*(1), 39–45.

MacLeod, L. (1987). *Battered but not beaten . . . Preventing wife battering in Canada*. Ottawa: Canadian Advisory Council on the Status of Women.

MacLeod, L. (1989). *Wife battering and the web of hope: Progress, dilemmas, and visions of prevention*. Ottawa: Health & Welfare Canada.

McCord, J. (1983). A forty year perspective on effects of child abuse and neglect. *Child Abuse and Neglect, 7*, 265–270.

McKay, E. J. (1987). *Children of battered women*. Paper presented at the Third National Family Violence Researchers' Conference, Durham, NH.

Mercer, S. L. (1987). *Not a pretty picture: An exploratory study of violence against women in high school dating relationships*. Unpublished data available from Education Wife Assault, Toronto, Ontario.

Miller, P., & Sperry, L. (1987). The socialization of anger and aggression. *Merrill-Palmer Quarterly, 33*, 1–31.

Ministry of the Attorney General. (1989). *Task force on mediation services*. Toronto, Ontario: Author.

Moore, D. M. (1979). *Battered women*. Beverly Hills, CA: Sage.

Mussen, P. H., & Conger, J. J. (1956). *Child development and personality*. New York: Harper.

Mussen, P. H., Conger, J. J., & Kagan, J. (1963). *Child development and personality* (2nd ed.). New York: Harper.

NiCarthy, G. (1982). *Getting free: A handbook for women in abusive relationships* (2nd ed.). Seattle: Seal Press.

O'Neill, D. (1989, July 18). Boy, 11, stabs man attacking his mother. *The Toronto Star*, p. 1.

Ontario Psychological Foundation. (1989). *In place of violence: Report of a public forum and workshop presented for secondary school students and teachers*. Toronto: Author.

Pagelow, M. D. (1984). *Family violence*. Toronto: Praeger.

Parry, R., Broder, E. A., Schmitt, E. A. G., Saunders, E. B., & Hood, E. (Eds.). (1986). *Custody disputes: Evaluation and intervention*. Toronto: Lexington.

Patterson, G. R. (1986). Performance models for antisocial boys. *American Psychologist, 41*, 432–444.

Patterson, G. R., DeBarysche, B. D., & Ramsey, E. (1989). A developmental perspective on antisocial behavior. *American Psychologist, 44*, 329–335.

Pepler, D., Moore, T. E., Mae, R., & Kates, M. (in press). The effects of exposure to family violence of children: New directions for research and intervention. In G. Cameron & M. Rothery (Eds.), *Family violence and neglect: Innovative interventions*. Toronto: Lawrence Erlbaum.

Pett, M. (1982). Correlates of children's social adjustment following divorce. *Journal of Divorce, 5*, 25–39.

Pfeffer, C. P., Plutchik, R., & Mizruchi, M. S. (1983). Suicidal and assaultive behavior in children: Classification, measurement and interrelations. *American Journal of Psychiatry, 140*, 154–157.

Pizzey, E. (1977). *Scream quietly or the neighbors will hear*. Short Hills, NJ: Ridley Enslow.

Porter, B., & O'Leary, K. D. (1980). Marital discord & childhood behavior problems. *Journal of Abnormal Psychology, 8*, 287–295.

Pynoos, R. S., & Eth, S. (1984). The child as witness to homicide. *Journal of Social Issues, 40*(2), 87–108.

Rae-Grant, N. I., Boyle, M. H., Offord, D. R., & Thomas, H. (1984). *The buffering effect of protective factors in reducing the incidence of common behavioral and emotional disorders in childhood*. Paper presented at the joint meeting of the American and Canadian Academies of Child Psychiatry, Toronto.

Rhodes, R. M., & Zelman, A. B. (1986). An ongoing multi-family group in a women's shelter. *American Journal of Orthopsychiatry, 56*(1), 120–130.

Roman, M., & Haddad, S. (1978). *The disposable parent*. New York: Holt, Rinehart & Winston.

Rosenbaum, A., & O'Leary, K. D. (1981). Children: The unintended victims of marital violence. *American Journal of Orthopsychiatry, 51*, 692–699.

Rosenberg, M. S. (1984). *Inter-generational family violence: A critique and implications for witnessing children*. Paper presented at the 92nd annual convention of the American Psychological Association, Toronto.

Rosewater, L. B. (1984, August). *The MMPI & battered women*. Paper presented at the Second Family Violence Researchers' Conference, Durham, NH.

Roy, M. (1977). *Battered women: A psychological study of domestic violence*. New York: Van Nostrand.

Rutter, M. (1971). Parent-child separation: Psychological effects on the children. *Journal of Child Psychology and Psychiatry and Applied Disciplines, 12*, 233–260.

Rutter, M. (1979). Protective factors in children's responses to stress and disadvantage. In M. W. Kent & J. E. Rolf (Eds.), *Primary prevention of psychopathology: Vol. 3. Promoting social competence and coping in children* (pp. 49–74). Hanover, NH: University Press of New England.

Rutter, M. (1983). Stress, coping, and development: Some issues and some questions. In N. Garmezy & M. Rutter (Eds.), *Stress, coping, and development in children* (pp. 1–41). New York: McGraw-Hill.

Rutter, M., & Giller, H. (1983). *Juvenile delinquency: Trends and perspectives*. New York: Guilford.

Sandler, I. N. (1980). Social support resources, stress and maladjustment of poor children. *American Journal of Community Psychology, 8*, 41–52.

Schechter, S., & Gary, L. T. (1988). In M. Straus (Ed.), *Abuse and victimization across the life span*. Baltimore: Johns Hopkins University Press.

Seligman, M. E. D. (1975). *Helplessness: On depression, development and death*. San Francisco: Freeman.

Seven deadly days. (1989, July 17). *Time*, p. 11.

Shaffer, P. R. (1988). *Social and personality development* (2nd ed.). Monterey, CA: Brooks/Cole.

Sinclair, D. (1985). *Understanding wife assault: A training manual for counselors and advocates*. Toronto: Ontario Government Bookstore.

Slater, E. J., & Haber, J. D. (1984). Adolescent adjustment following divorce as a function of familial conflict. *Journal of Consulting and Clinical Psychology, 52*, 920–921.

Sonkin, D. J., Martin, D., & Walker, L. E. (1985). *The male batterer: A treatment approach*. New York: Springer.

Sopp-Gilson, S. (1980). Children from violent homes. *Journal of Ontario Association of Children's Aid Societies, 23*(10), 1–5.

Sroufe, L. A., & Fleeson, J. (1986). Attachment and the construction of relationships. In W. W. Hartup & Z. Rubin (Eds.), *Relationships and development* (pp. 51–72). Hillsdale, NJ: Lawrence Erlbaum.

Standing Senate Committee on Health, Welfare, and Science. (1980). *Child at risk*. Hull, Quebec: Minister of Supply and Services, Canada.

Stark, E., Flitcraft, A., Zuckerman, D., Grey, A. J., & Frazier, W. (1981, April). Wife abuse in the medical setting: An introduction for health personnel. *Domestic Violence, Monograph Series, 1*, 1–54.

Stavrou-Petersen, K., & Gamache, D. (1988). *My family and me: Violence free: A domestic violence prevention curriculum*. St. Paul: Minnesota Coalition for Battered Women.

Stone, L. J., & Church, J. (1957). *Childhood and adolescence: A psychology of the growing person*. New York: Random House.

Stone, L. J., & Church, J. (1968). *Childhood and adolescence: A psychology of the growing person* (2nd ed.). New York: Random House.

Stone, L. J., & Church, J. (1973). *Childhood and adolescence: A psychology of the growing person* (3rd ed.). New York: Random House.

Straus, M. A., Gelles, R. J., & Steinmetz, S. (1980). *Behind closed doors*. Doubleday, Anchor.

Stullman, M. E., Schoenenberger, A., & Hanks, S. E. (1987, July 8). *Assessment and treatment of the child witness of martial violence*. Paper presented at the Family and Violence Research Conference, University of New Hampshire, Durham.

Thorpe, L. P. (1946). *Child psychology and development*. New York: Ronald.

Toufexis, A. (1987, December 21). Home is where the hurt is: Wife beating among the well-to-do is no longer a secret. *Time, 130*(25), 68.

Van der Kolk, B. A. (1987). The psychological consequences of overwhelming life experiences. In B. A. Van der Kolk (Ed.), *Psychological trauma*. Washington, DC: American Psychiatric Press.

Walker, L. (1979). *Battered women*. New York: Harper & Row.

Walker, L. E. (1989). Psychology and violence against women. *American Psychologist, 44*, 695–702.

Walker, L. E., & Edwall, G. E. (1987). Domestic violence and determination of visitation and custody in divorce. In D. J. Sonkin (Ed.), *Domestic violence on trial: Psychological and legal dimensions of family violence* (pp. 127–152). New York: Springer.

Wallerstein, J. (1983). Children of divorce: The psychological tasks of the child. *American Journal of Orthopsychiatry, 53*, 230–243.
Wallerstein, J. S., & Kelly, J. B. (1975). The effects of parental divorce: Experiences of the preschool child. *Journal of the American Academy of Child Psychiatry, 14*, 600–616.
Wallerstein, J. S., & Kelly, J. B. (1980). The effects of parental divorce: Experiences of the child in later latency. *American Journal of Orthopsychiatry, 50*, 256–269.
Watson, M. (1986). *Children of domestic violence: Programs and treatment*. Prepared for the office for the Prevention of Family Violence, Alberta Social Services, Edmonton, Alberta.
Weintraub, S., Liebert, D., & Neale, J. M. (1978). Teacher ratings of child and his family. In E. J. Anthony (Ed.), *The child and his family: Vol. 4. Vulnerable children* (pp. 335–346). New York: John Wiley.
Weintraub, S., Prinz, R., & Neale, J. M. (1975). Peer evaluations of the competence of children vulnerable to psychopathology. *Journal of Abnormal Child Psychology, 6*, 461–473.
Wellman, B. (1981). Applying network analysis to the study of support. In B. Gottlieb (Ed.), *Social networks and social support*. Beverly Hills, CA: Sage.
West, M. O., & Prinz, R. J. (1987). Parental alcoholism and childhood psychopathology. *Psychological Bulletin, 102*, 204–218.
Widom, C. S. (1989). Does violence beget violence? A critical examination of the literature. *Psychological Bulletin, 106*, 3–28.
Wilson, S., Cameron, S., Jaffe, P., & Wolfe, D. (1989). Children exposed to wife abuse: An intervention model. *Social Casework: The Journal of Contemporary Social Work, 70*, 180–184.
Wolfe, D. A. (1987). *Child abuse: Implications for child development and psychopathology*. Newbury Park, CA: Sage.
Wolfe, D. A., Jaffe, P., Wilson, S., & Zak, L. (1985). Children of battered women: The relation of child behavior to family violence and maternal stress. *Journal of Consulting and Clinical Psychology, 53*, 657–665.
Wolfe, D. A., & Wolfe, V. V. (1988). The sexually abused child. In E. J. Mash & L. G. Terdal (Eds.), *Behavioral assessment of childhood disorders* (2nd ed., pp. 670–714). New York: Guilford.
Wolfe, D. A., Zak, L., Wilson, S., & Jaffe, P. (1986). Child witnesses to violence between parents: Critical issues in behavioral and social adjustment. *Journal of Abnormal Child Psychology, 14*(1), 95–104.
Woods, F. B. (1981). *Living without violence*. Fayetteville, AK: Project for Victims of Domestic Violence.
Young v. Young, 14 R.F.L. (3rd) 222 (N.B.Q.B. 1986).

INDEX

ABOUT THE AUTHORS

Peter Jaffe is Director of the London Family Court Clinic and Adjunct Associate Professor in the departments of psychology and psychiatry at the University of Western Ontario, in London, Ontario, Canada. He completed his training in psychology at McGill University and the University of Western Ontario, where he received his doctorate in clinical psychology. He was a founding member of several community organizations related to family violence, including the Battered Women's Advocacy Clinic, the Family Consultant Service of the London Police Force, the London Custody and Access Project, and the London Coordinating Committee on Family Violence. Since 1980, he has been actively pursuing primary prevention programming in this area as part of his role as Trustee of the London Board of Education. He is on the editorial board of *Canadian Psychology* and has served as guest editor for a special issue of the *Canadian Journal of Community Mental Health* on the topic of wife battering in Canada. He has written numerous chapters and journal articles on the topics of wife abuse, custody disputes, delinquent youth, and children of battered women.

David A. Wolfe (Ph.D., University of South Florida) is Associate Professor of Psychology and Psychiatry and Co-Director of Clinical Training at the University of Western Ontario, and Director of Research at the Institute for the Prevention of Child Abuse in Toronto. He holds a Diplomate in Clinical Psychology from the American Board of Professional Psychology and has an active consulting practice with the Children's Aid Society of London/Middlesex. He serves on the boards of the Family Consultant Service Management Committee and the Child Witness Preparation Program in London and has active interests in the assessment and prevention of child maltreatment. He has been a member of the editorial boards of *Child Abuse and Neglect, Delinquencia, Journal of Family Violence, Journal of Clinical Psychiatry*, and the *Journal of Consulting and Clinical Psychology* and has written extensively on the topics of physical and sexual abuse of children. He is coauthor (with K. Kaufman, J. Aragona, and J. Sandler) of *The Child Management Program for Abusive Parents* and author of *Child Abuse: Implications for Child Development and Psychopathology*.

Susan Kaye Wilson is completing her Ph.D. in clinical child psychology at the University of Western Ontario, having completed her internship training in 1989 at the London Family Court Clinic and Madame Vanier Children's Services. She has been actively involved in developing group counseling programs for children of battered women in five different communities in southwestern Ontario. She has also been instrumental in the development of a court preparation program for child sexual abuse victims who have to testify in court proceedings. She has written many journal articles on the topic of assessment and intervention strategies for children of battered women.

NOTES

NOTES

NOTES

NOTES